ROSE GUIDE TO THE BOOK OF ACTS

Rose Guide to the Book of Acts

Published by Rose Publishing
An imprint of Tyndale House Ministries
Carol Stream, Illinois
www.hendricksonrose.com

ISBN 978-164938-020-3

Contributing authors: Len Woods (Chapters 1, 6); Cyndi Parker (Chapter 3); Carl Simmons, Jessica Curiel (Chapter 4); Sarah Welch (Chapter 5).

Chapter 3 is partially adapted from "The Threefold Expansion of the Early Church: Jerusalem, Judea, and Samaria" by Cyndi Parker in *Lexham Geographic Commentary: Acts Through Revelation.* Edited by Barry Beizel and Kristopher Lyle. (Lexham Press, 2018, 2019). Used by permission.

Printed in the United States of America
010821VP

CONTENTS

CHAPTER 1

The Story of Acts 5

CHAPTER 2

The Book of Acts 27

CHAPTER 3

The World of the First Christians 43

CHAPTER 4

Life of Paul 65

CHAPTER 5

Who's Who in the Book of Acts 95

CHAPTER 6

The Holy Spirit 123

CHAPTER 1

The Story of Acts

Jesus' disciples were riding a roller coaster of emotions and insights. First there was the hope and expectation raised by Jesus' life and ministry. Then it all seemed to go so wrong with his horrible death—only to turn right side up once and for all with his resurrection. But the disciples' newfound joy lasted only a few weeks when they saw their Lord ascend to heaven and leave them behind. Yet the Lord had promised to them the Holy Spirit—one who would come with power and guide them "into all the truth" (John 16:13).

This small and confused group of disciples gathered together in one place in Jerusalem to pray and seek the Lord's guidance. When the Holy Spirit overpowered the place with a sound like a roaring windstorm and what seemed like tongues of fire, history changed forever. The Spirit set Jerusalem ablaze, and the good news of Jesus Christ spread like wildfire.

So begins the story of the church in the book of Acts. This New Testament book, traditionally known as *Acts of the Apostles*, records the narrative of the first Christians who carried forward the life-changing mission that Jesus had given to them.

THE STORY OF ACTS AT A GLANCE

The Holy Spirit at Pentecost (Acts 1–3)

The first event recorded in the book of Acts is Christ's ascension into heaven. Before he departed, he told his closest disciples what would happen to them:

> You will receive power when the Holy Spirit comes on you; and you will be my witnesses in Jerusalem, and in all Judea and Samaria, and to the ends of the earth.
>
> ACTS 1:8

In this one Bible verse, we get the basic story line of Acts. Who will receive this power? "You"—all who are disciples of Jesus. What will they be empowered to do? "Be my witnesses"—testify about all they experienced with Jesus and share the gospel of God's forgiveness and love. When will this happen? "When the Holy Spirit comes." Where will this happen? Firstly, they'll be witnesses "in Jerusalem," then "Judea and Samaria," and they won't stop until they get to "the ends of the earth."

As instructed, the disciples got to work, praying and waiting in Jerusalem. But they didn't have to wait long. While Jews and converts to Judaism from all over were gathered in Jerusalem for the festival of Pentecost, the Holy Spirit of God came upon the followers of Jesus like a hurricane!

> Suddenly a sound like the blowing of a violent wind came from heaven and filled the whole house where they were sitting. They saw what seemed to be tongues of fire that separated and came to rest on each of them. All of them were filled with the Holy Spirit and began to speak in other tongues as the Spirit enabled them.
>
> ACTS 2:2–4

Pentecost by Duccio di Buoninsegna (c. 1308)

The believers were empowered to share the truth of God with all those foreign visitors in languages that they themselves had never learned! The apostle Peter seized the moment and gave a short sermon to the crowd about Christ's death and resurrection. As a result, three thousand people repented of their sins, put their faith in Jesus, and were baptized.

This new spiritual community, called the church, was fiercely devoted to the apostles' teaching. They ate together and helped one another financially. They shared a common faith, life, and mission. They worshiped wholeheartedly, prayed fervently, and saw God do miraculous things through the apostles. As a result, the whole city of Jerusalem was in awe. More and more Jews believed in Jesus as the Messiah.

Now there were staying in Jerusalem God-fearing Jews from every nation under heaven. ... **Parthians, Medes** and **Elamites**; residents of **Mesopotamia, Judea** and **Cappadocia, Pontus** and **Asia, Phrygia** and **Pamphylia, Egypt** and the parts of **Libya** near Cyrene; visitors from **Rome** (both Jews and converts to Judaism); **Cretans** and **Arabs** [saying], "We hear them declaring the wonders of God in our own tongues!"

ACTS 2:5, 9–11

Persecution and the Church (Acts 4–9)

Not surprisingly, this rapid, new movement was soon met with backlash. Peter and John were arrested and brought before the Sanhedrin, the same group that only weeks before had condemned Jesus to death (Matt. 26:59–68). Filled with the Holy Spirit, Peter was fearless! Peter boldly preached the gospel to them, declaring that "salvation is found in no one else" besides Jesus (Acts 4:12). He insisted that he and the apostles would never stop sharing this truth. It was just as Jesus had told them:

> When you are brought before synagogues, rulers and authorities, do not worry about how you will defend yourselves or what you will say, for the Holy Spirit will teach you at that time what you should say.
>
> LUKE 12:11–12

Threatened and released, Peter and John ramped up their efforts to share the good news, and the church continued to grow. The more the Jewish leaders cracked down, the more the church spoke up. Nothing could deter Christ's followers, not threats, floggings, or even death. One church leader, Stephen, was dragged outside Jerusalem and stoned to death for testifying about Jesus. Stephen's death sparked a wave of violent persecution against the church.

The Stoning of St. Stephen fresco in St. Cyril and Methodius, Prague

Believers in Jesus fled Jerusalem in droves. But ironically, this only meant that the gospel was advancing. Opposition in Jerusalem sent them into Judea and Samaria, just as Jesus had said would happen (Acts 1:8). Philip preached the gospel in Samaria and then to an Ethiopian official the Lord led him to on a road in Judea. The man trusted in Jesus and was immediately baptized. The road the official was traveling on led to Gaza, a port city from where he'd presumably travel to Africa. The Great Commission Jesus had given his followers—"to make disciples of all nations"—was just beginning (Matt. 28:19).

One of the chief engineers of the persecution campaign against the church was a young man named Saul (also called Paul). After Stephen was martyred in Jerusalem (Saul had been there for that; Acts 7:58; 8:1), Saul set his sights on Damascus, a city northeast of Jerusalem. He was headed to Damascus to arrest believers in Jesus who had fled the persecution in Jerusalem. A great light flashed from heaven, he fell to the ground, and the risen Lord revealed the truth: "I am Jesus, whom you are persecuting" (Acts 9:5). Physically blinded by the experience, Saul arrived in Damascus where the Lord directed a man named Ananias to go to him and restore his sight. Confronted, then converted by Jesus, Saul joined the very movement he had tried to abolish.

Peter's Mission (Acts 10–12)

Meanwhile, God was using the apostle Peter to open the door of salvation—and of the church—to those outside the Jewish community. Even some in the church, like Peter, didn't fully understand that the power of the gospel was for all people, no matter who they were in society or where they came from. So God sent Peter to the home of Cornelius, a Roman centurion and a gentile. There, Peter saw the Holy Spirit fill the gentile believers, and was convinced:

> I now realize how true it is that God does not show favoritism but accepts from every nation the one who fears him and does what is right.
>
> ACTS 10:34–35

Soon, there was a growing and thriving community of gentile believers in Antioch of Syria (Acts 11:19–30). In fact, it was in this city that the followers of Jesus were first called Christians, and it was from here that Saul (Paul) began launching missionary efforts to reach the world with the gospel.

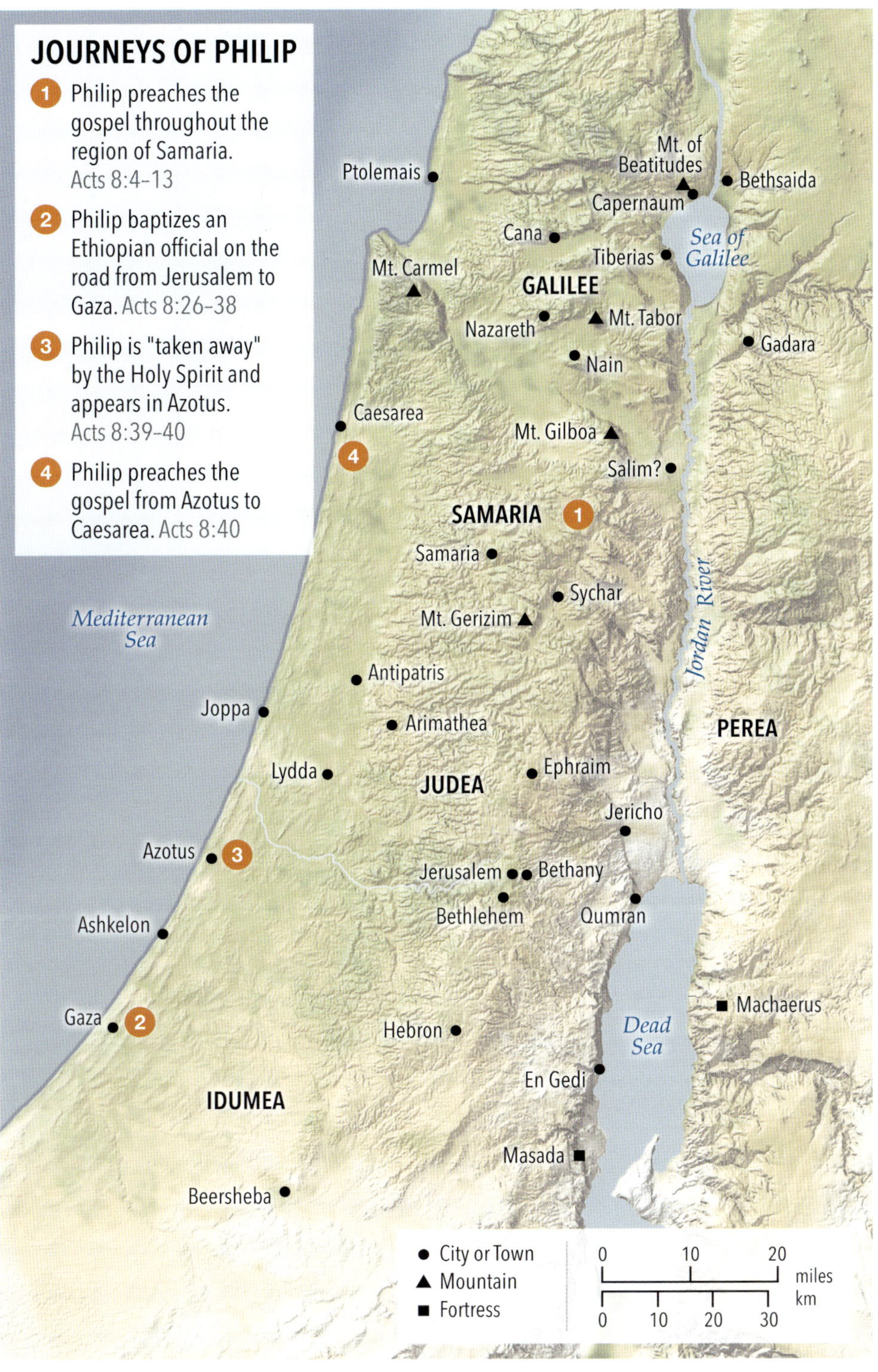
JOURNEYS OF PHILIP
1 Philip preaches the gospel throughout the region of Samaria. Acts 8:4–13
2 Philip baptizes an Ethiopian official on the road from Jerusalem to Gaza. Acts 8:26–38
3 Philip is "taken away" by the Holy Spirit and appears in Azotus. Acts 8:39–40
4 Philip preaches the gospel from Azotus to Caesarea. Acts 8:40
Ptolemais
Mt. of Beatitudes
Bethsaida
Capernaum
Cana
Sea of Galilee
Tiberias
Mt. Carmel
GALILEE
Nazareth
Mt. Tabor
Gadara
Nain
Caesarea
Mt. Gilboa
Salim?
SAMARIA
Samaria
Sychar
Mt. Gerizim
Mediterranean Sea
Jordan River
Antipatris
Joppa
Arimathea
PEREA
Lydda
JUDEA
Ephraim
Jericho
Azotus
Jerusalem
Bethany
Ashkelon
Bethlehem
Qumran
Machaerus
Gaza
Hebron
Dead Sea
En Gedi
IDUMEA
Masada
Beersheba
City or Town
Mountain
Fortress
0 10 20 miles
0 10 20 30 km

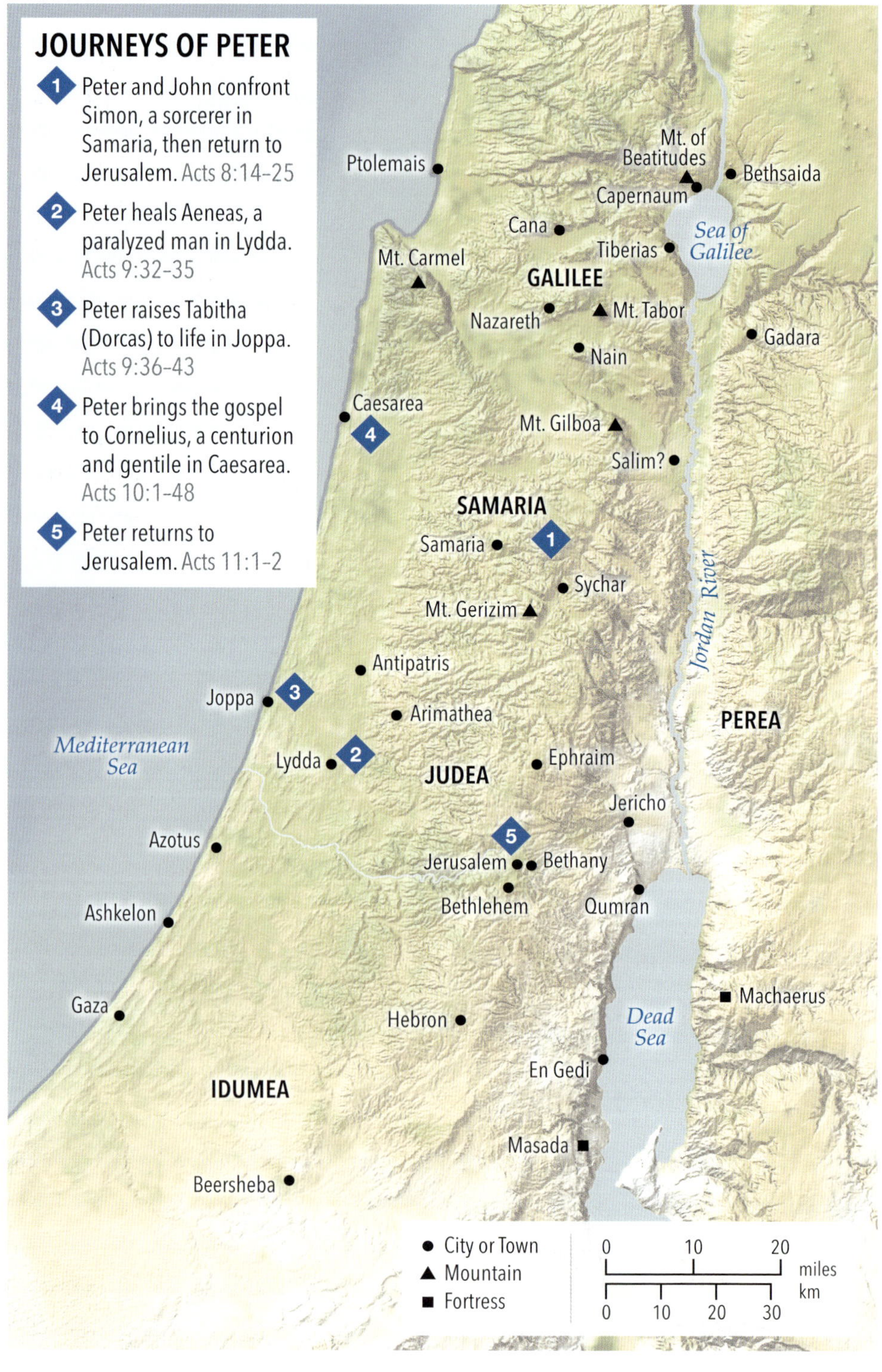
JOURNEYS OF PETER
1 Peter and John confront Simon, a sorcerer in Samaria, then return to Jerusalem. Acts 8:14-25
2 Peter heals Aeneas, a paralyzed man in Lydda. Acts 9:32-35
3 Peter raises Tabitha (Dorcas) to life in Joppa. Acts 9:36-43
4 Peter brings the gospel to Cornelius, a centurion and gentile in Caesarea. Acts 10:1-48
5 Peter returns to Jerusalem. Acts 11:1-2
Ptolemais
Mt. of Beatitudes
Bethsaida
Capernaum
Cana
Sea of Galilee
Tiberias
Mt. Carmel
GALILEE
Nazareth
Mt. Tabor
Gadara
Nain
Caesarea
Mt. Gilboa
Salim?
SAMARIA
Samaria
Sychar
Jordan River
Mt. Gerizim
Antipatris
Joppa
Arimathea
PEREA
Mediterranean Sea
Lydda
JUDEA
Ephraim
Jericho
Azotus
Jerusalem
Bethany
Bethlehem
Qumran
Ashkelon
Machaerus
Gaza
Hebron
Dead Sea
En Gedi
IDUMEA
Masada
Beersheba
City or Town
Mountain
Fortress
0 10 20 miles
0 10 20 30 km

Paul's Mission (Acts 13–28)

About half of the chapters in Acts focus on Paul's journeys. For his first missionary outreach, Paul teamed up with Barnabas and for a short time with John Mark. By the Holy Spirit's leading, they took the gospel to the island of Cyprus, then to cities in the south-central region of Asia Minor (modern-day Turkey). Everywhere Paul went, it seemed there was either a riot or a revival—sometimes both! He typically visited local synagogues first, where he almost always encountered opposition. Next, he shared God's truth with gentiles, who were often more receptive.

Between Paul's first and second missionary journeys, he went to Jerusalem, which was at that time the main locale of the Christian church. There, church leaders like James, John, Peter, and others dealt with the question of how to incorporate gentiles into a largely Jewish church. In what came to be known as the Jerusalem Council, they concluded that non-Jews were just as much a part of the church as Jews and that they would not be required to follow Jewish religious laws.

On Paul's second missionary journey, he was accompanied by Silas, and they were later joined by Timothy, Luke, and a husband-and-wife team, Priscilla and Aquila. Paul headed north and then west through Asia Minor and Greece, this apostolic team strengthening believers and establishing churches everywhere they went. It was on this journey that Paul explained the gospel to philosophers in Athens.

On his third journey, Paul retraced his steps, revisiting cities he had previously evangelized and church congregations he had helped plant. During a two-year layover in Ephesus, God did extraordinary things through Paul, and many throughout the region came to faith.

Later, when Paul was in Jerusalem, he was falsely accused of defiling the temple, arrested, and sent to prison. He was held in prison two years awaiting trial. Nevertheless, he shared his faith with various high-ranking officials while he waited in chains. Paul was eventually put on a ship headed to Rome to appeal his case to Caesar. This journey would be the farthest he had traveled—to Rome, the epicenter of the Greco-Roman world, far from where the church had begun in Jerusalem, Judea, and Samaria (Acts 1:8).

When he arrived in Rome, Paul was placed under house arrest to await yet another trial. This is where the narrative of Acts ends, with Paul using the difficult situation he was in as an opportunity to tell others about salvation in Jesus:

> For two whole years Paul stayed there in his own rented house and welcomed all who came to see him. He proclaimed the kingdom of God and taught about the Lord Jesus Christ—with all boldness and without hindrance!
>
> ACTS 28:30–31

Rome

10 Key Bible Verses in Acts

1. But you will receive power when the Holy Spirit comes on you; and you will be my witnesses in Jerusalem, and in all Judea and Samaria, and to the ends of the earth. —ACTS 1:8

2. Peter replied, "Repent and be baptized, every one of you, in the name of Jesus Christ for the forgiveness of your sins. And you will receive the gift of the Holy Spirit." —ACTS 2:38

3. They devoted themselves to the apostles' teaching and to fellowship, to the breaking of bread and to prayer. —ACTS 2:42

4. Salvation is found in no one else, for there is no other name under heaven given to mankind by which we must be saved. —ACTS 4:12

5. Peter and the other apostles replied: "We must obey God rather than human beings!" —ACTS 5:29

6. Then Peter began to speak: "I now realize how true it is that God does not show favoritism but accepts from every nation the one who fears him and does what is right." —ACTS 10:34–35

7. They replied, "Believe in the Lord Jesus, and you will be saved—you and your household." —ACTS 16:31

8. Now the Berean Jews were of more noble character than those in Thessalonica, for they received the message with great eagerness and examined the Scriptures every day to see if what Paul said was true. —ACTS 17:11

9. Keep watch over yourselves and all the flock of which the Holy Spirit has made you overseers. Be shepherds of the church of God, which he bought with his own blood. —ACTS 20:28

10. And now what are you waiting for? Get up, be baptized and wash your sins away, calling on his name. —ACTS 22:16

THE BOOK OF ACTS IN BIBLICAL HISTORY

When Adam and Eve rebelled in the garden of Eden, God began a rescue mission. He wanted to restore his fallen world and creatures so they could fulfill his original intentions for them: to enjoy him and praise him forever. Throughout history, God has shaped events to bring about his plans of renewal.

While God is the force, mind, and will behind the mission, he has chosen humans to work alongside him. The stories in the book of Acts reveal how

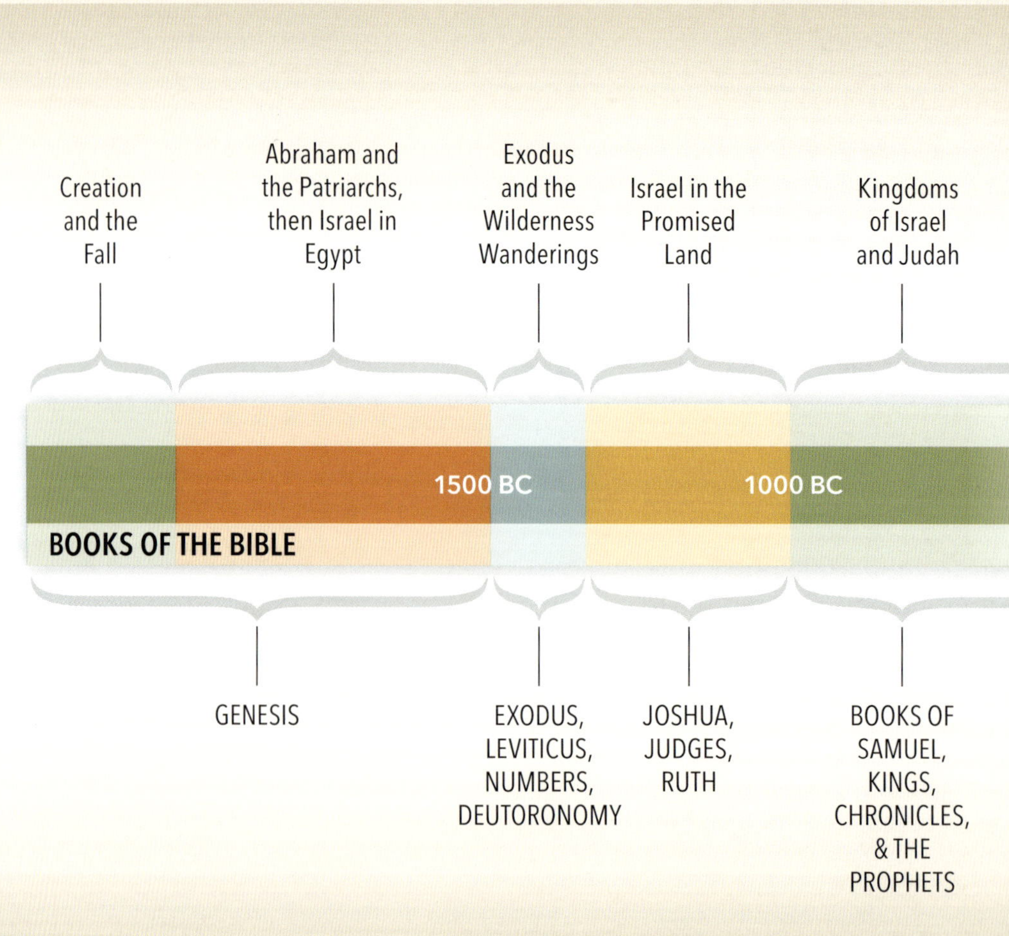

God is moving his mission forward. This is picked up from the ending of the gospel of Luke, where the apostles are commissioned to be part of that mission: "You are witnesses of these things" (Luke 24:48). Empowered by the Holy Spirit, Jesus' disciples became an extension of God's plans to reach the whole world: "witnesses … to the ends of the earth" (Acts 1:8). The story of the church becomes the story of the fulfillment of God's mission to make all things new.

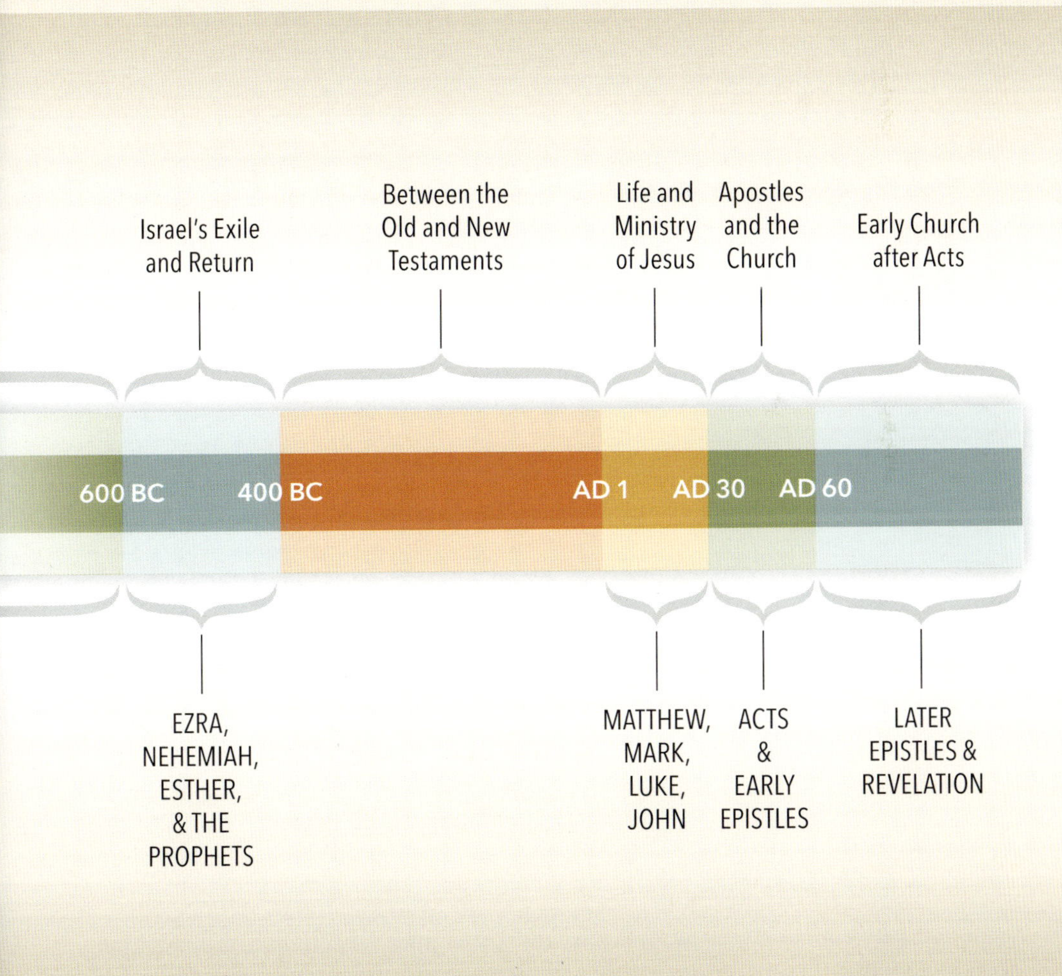

BOOK OF ACTS TIME LINE

- **CAESAR AUGUSTUS** rules the Roman Empire. 27 BC–AD 14
- **JESUS CHRIST** is born in Bethlehem. c. 4 BC*
- **HEROD THE GREAT** dies. 4 BC
- **HEROD ANTIPAS** governs Galilee and Perea. 4 BC–AD 39
- **PAUL** (Saul) is born. c. 5

30 BC | AD 1 | AD 10

KEY

c. **APPROXIMATE DATE** (*circa*)

 **BOOK OF THE BIBLE** (Date ranges indicate a time frame in which the book is believed to have been written.)

✠ **EVENT IN THE BOOK OF ACTS** (If no date is listed, the date is unknown.)

*Bible scholars date the birth of Christ between 6 and 4 BC. This time line follows a 4 BC date.

- **PONTIUS PILATE** governs Judea. 26–36
- **BAPTISM:** John the Baptist baptizes Jesus. c. 27
- **MINISTRY:** Jesus gathers disciples, teaches, heals, performs miracles, and raises the dead. c. 27–30
- **HEROD ANTIPAS** imprisons and executes John the Baptist.
- **DEATH AND RESURRECTION:** Jesus is crucified and raised from the dead. c. 30
- ✠ **ASCENSION:** Jesus ascends to heaven. c. 30 Acts 1:6–9
- ✠ **MATTIAS** is chosen as an apostle to replace Judas Iscariot. c. 30 Acts 1:15–26

AD 20 | AD 30 | AD 35

- **EMPEROR TIBERIUS** rules the Roman Empire. 17–37
- ✠ **PENTECOST:** Holy Spirit fills believers. c. 30 Acts 2:1–41
- ✠ **CHURCH IN JERUSALEM** is established. c. 30–32 Acts 2:42–47
- ✠ **PETER AND JOHN** perform miracles and face persecution. c. 30 Acts 3:1–5:21
- ✠ **STEPHEN** is martyred in Jerusalem. c. 32 Acts 7:54–60
- ✠ **PERSECUTION** forces believers to disperse from Jerusalem. Acts 8:4
- ✠ **PHILIP** preaches in Samaria. Acts 8:5–25
- ✠ **PHILIP** baptizes and Ethiopian official. Acts 8:26–39

CONVERSION: Paul encounters Christ on the road to Damascus. c. 37 Acts 9:1-19

HEROD AGRIPPA governs Galilee, Perea, and Judea. 37–44

PAUL goes to Arabia. Gal. 1:17

PAUL travels to Damascus, Jerusalem, Caesarea, and finally Tarsus. Acts 9:26–30

CALIGULA rules the Roman Empire. 37–41

HEROD ANTIPAS is exiled, where he later dies. 39

AD 35 AD 40

PETER brings the gospel to Cornelius. c. 40 Acts 10:1–48

CLAUDIUS assassinates Caligula to become the emperor. 41

CLAUDIUS rules the Roman Empire. 41–54

BARNABAS brings Paul to the church in Antioch of Syria. Acts 11:25-26

BELIEVERS in Jesus Christ are first called Christians in Antioch of Syria. Acts 11:26

SEVERE FAMINE in Judea. 44–48

PAUL AND BARNABAS deliver funds to believers in Jerusalem facing a famine. Acts 11:27-30

APOSTLE JAMES (brother of John) is martyred in Jerusalem by Herod Agrippa. 44 Acts 12:2

PETER is imprisoned by Herod Agrippa but miraculously escapes. 44 Acts 12:3–19

HEROD AGRIPPA dies. 44 Acts 12:20–23

PAUL'S FIRST MISSIONARY JOURNEY: Accompanied by Barnabas and John Mark; travels as far as Cyprus and Pisidia. c. 47–49 Acts 13:1–14:28

IN LYSTRA, the people attempt to worship Paul and Barnabas as gods, then later stone Paul to near death. Acts 14:8–20

AD 45 AD 50

GALATIANS: Paul writes to the churches in Galatia. c. 49

JERUSALEM COUNCIL concludes that gentile Christians are not required to obey Jewish religious laws. c. 49 Acts 15:1–35

HEROD AGRIPPA II governs territories in Syria, Galilee, and Perea. 49–92

CLAUDIUS expels Jews from Rome. 49

PAUL'S SECOND MISSIONARY JOURNEY: Accompanied by Silas, Timothy, Luke, Priscilla, and Aquila; travels as far as Macedonia and Greece. c. 49–51 Acts 15:36–18:22

BARNABAS AND JOHN MARK minister in Cyprus. Acts 15:39

GOSPEL OF MARK: John Mark writes his gospel. c. 50s

LYDIA becomes a Christian in Philippi. Acts 16:12-15

MARS HILL SERMON: Paul shares the gospel with philosophers in Athens. Acts 17:16-34

PAUL MEETS TIMOTHY in Lystra. Acts 16:1-3

1 AND 2 THESSALONIANS: Paul writes letters to the church in Thessalonica. c. 50–52

1 AND 2 CORINTHIANS: Paul writes to believers in Corinth. c. 55–57

PAUL meets fellow tentmakers Priscilla and Aquila in Corinth. c. 51 Acts 18:1-13

PAUL appears before Gallio, governor of Achaia, in Corinth. c. 51 Acts 18:12-17

AD 50 — AD 55

FELIX becomes Roman governor (procurator) of Judea. 52

PAUL'S THIRD MISSIONARY JOURNEY: Accompanied by Timothy and Luke; travels as far as Macedonia and Greece. c. 52–57 Acts 18:23-21:26

APOLLOS ministers in Achaia. Acts 18:27-28

EPHESUS: Paul spends two years in Ephesus. Acts 19:8-10

CLAUDIUS is poisoned to death by his wife. 54

NERO becomes emperor at age sixteen. 54

NERO rules the Roman Empire. 54–68

FESTUS becomes governor (procurator) of Judea. 59

PAUL appears before Festus, Herod Agrippa II, and Bernice. c. 59 Acts 25:13–26:32

PAUL appeals his case to Caesar, and so is sent to Rome. c. 59 Acts 27:1

PAUL'S JOURNEY TO ROME c. 59–60 Acts 27:1–28:16

MALTA: Paul is shipwrecked on his way to Rome. c. 59 Acts 27:27–28:11

ROMANS: Paul writes his most theological epistle, the letter to the church in Rome. c. 57

ROME: Paul spends two years under house arrest in Rome. 60–62 Acts 28:30–31

AD 60

PAUL arrives in Jerusalem where he is arrested. c. 57 Acts 21:30–33

PAUL appears before the Sanhedrin, then Felix and Drusilla. c. 57 Acts 22:30–23:10

PAUL spends two years in prison in awaiting trial. c. 57–59 Acts 24:24–26

GOSPEL OF LUKE AND ACTS: Luke writes his gospel and the book of Acts. c. 60–62

GOSPEL OF MATTHEW: Matthew writes his gospel. c. 60s

EPHESIANS, PHILIPPIANS, COLOSSIANS, AND PHILEMON: While in Rome, Paul writes to churches. c. 60–62

JAMES the brother of Jesus is martyred. 62

Paul is released and travels throughout the Mediterranean. c. 62–64

1 TIMOTHY: Paul writes his first letter to Timothy, a pastor in Ephesus. c. 62–66

1 AND 2 PETER: Peter writes two epistles. c. 64–65

TITUS: Paul writes to Titus, a pastor in Crete. c. 64–66

- **NERO** blames Christians for a massive fire in Rome and persecutes them. 64–68

- **PAUL** is imprisoned in Rome. c. 64

2 TIMOTHY: Paul writes his final epistle. c. 66–67

- **JEWISH REVOLT:** An uprising against the Romans begins in Jerusalem. 66

AD 70

- **PAUL AND PETER** are martyred in Rome. c. 66–68

- **NERO** commits suicide after the Roman Senate condemns him. 68

- **VESPASIAN** rules the Roman Empire. 69–79

- **TEMPLE** in Jerusalem is destroyed by the Romans. 70

- **MASADA** falls to the Romans. 73

TITUS rules the Roman Empire. 79–81

DOMITIAN rules the Roman Empire. 81–96

1, 2, AND 3 JOHN AND REVELATION:
John writes his epistles and the book of Revelation. 85–90

JOHN, after exile on Patmos, dies in Ephesus. 100

AD 80 | AD 90 | AD 100

CHAPTER 2

The Book of Acts

Together, the gospel of Luke and the book of Acts form something of a "two-volume set" of the story of Jesus Christ and his church. In Luke, we meet Jesus of Nazareth acting through the power of the Holy Spirit. As the promised Messiah, Jesus' life, ministry, and death on the cross fulfill God's promises and bring good news to all people from all walks of life. The narrative of Acts begins where the gospel of Luke leaves off, with the resurrected Christ. In Acts, the biblical writer continues the story about God's work in history, telling his readers how the first Christians advanced the mission that Jesus launched.

WHO WROTE THE BOOK OF ACTS?

An early church tradition names Luke as the author of Acts, as well as the gospel that bears his name. Determining the authorship of an anonymous text like Acts can be very difficult. However, there is enough internal evidence between the two books and Paul's epistles to make Luke a plausible candidate. For instance, Acts 28:16 suggests that the author of the book came to Rome with Paul. From Paul's epistles written from Rome, a list of those who were with him there can be assembled: Epaphras, Epaphroditus, Timothy, Tychicus, Aristarchus, Mark, Demas, Jesus-Justus, and Luke.

- The first two did not arrive with Paul when he came to Rome.
- The next four on the list can be ruled out because the author mentions them by name in Acts.
- Demas deserted Paul later, which makes him an unlikely candidate.
- No church tradition exists in favor of authorship by Jesus-Justus as there is for Luke.
- Some medical terminology appears in both the gospel of Luke and the book of Acts, and Paul mentions a "Luke" in Colossians 4:14 who was a physician, bolstering the conclusion that Luke is the author of Acts.

One interesting detail in Acts is the proper use of specific titles for various Roman officials. This could not have been done easily by someone writing many years after the events of Acts, since provincial boundaries and terms frequently changed. The use of these titles suggests the author was an eyewitness, someone with firsthand knowledge.

TITLE	IN ACTS	DESCRIPTION
Proconsul *anthypatos*	Used of Sergius Paulus of Cyprus and Gallio of Achaia (Acts 13:7; 18:12).	This is the title for a ruler of a Roman senatorial province.
Magistrates *stratēgoi*	Used of the authorities in Philippi, a Roman colony (Acts 16:20, 22, 35, 37–38).	Though the technical Roman term for those in charge of a colony was *duumviri*, Luke used a popular local term, showing his familiarity with the area.
City Officials *politarchēs*	Used of the leaders of the city of Thessalonica (Acts 17:6, 8).	This strange term was thought to be an error, until an inscription on the city gate was unearthed using the same word.
Clerk *grammateus*	Used of an official in Ephesus (Acts 19:35).	This is the same word used in other places for *scribe*. In Ephesus, it meant the town recorder.
Governor *hēgemōn*	Used of Felix and Festus (Acts 23:24, 26, 33; 24:1, 10; 26:30).	Title for the ruler of an imperial province or a ruler with authority from the emperor.
Chief Official *prōtos*	Used of Publius, governor of the island of Malta (Acts 28:7).	This term might seem like a generic term, but inscriptions found on the island of Malta show it was the specific title used there.

WHEN WAS ACTS WRITTEN?

The book of Acts ends with Paul spending two years under house arrest in Rome, about AD 60–62. Paul's later epistles indicate that he eventually left Rome and traveled elsewhere in the Mediterranean sharing the gospel. This seemingly cliffhanger ending to Acts with Paul being held in Rome suggests that the gospel of Luke and then Acts were written during or shortly after AD 60–62. Some Bible scholars, however, place the writing of Acts much later in the first century, so the book's conclusion in Rome then would be a natural literary stopping point, with Paul and the gospel having reached the epicenter of the Roman world.

WHO WAS ACTS WRITTEN FOR?

Both the books of Luke and Acts address a person named Theophilus. He is called "most excellent" (Luke 1:3), a common way of addressing socially important people. Some Bible scholars have suggested that Theophilus was a Roman noble, perhaps a member of the government. Others think that he could have been a Christian convert who became Luke's patron. Books in the first century were expensive, and few people could afford them. It was common for a wealthy patron to finance books and then grant others access to read them. If Theophilus was Luke's patron, then it's possible that he financed Luke's writing, paid for copies of the books, and gave churches access to them.

Acts was meant for several audiences:

- Firstly, the book is addressed to an individual, Theophilus.
- Secondly, it's for other people like Theophilus, perhaps Romans who were intrigued by Christianity.
- Thirdly, it's for all Christian believers, Jews and gentiles alike.

WHY WAS ACTS WRITTEN?

Acts is not an academic history book, simply recording facts of the early church. Rather, Luke presents this history selectively to get across key messages to readers. Luke records specific stories of the first Christians for four important purposes.

1. Proclamation Purpose

The book of Acts proclaims the good news of Jesus. In the narration of events and in the speeches in Acts, we find a basic presentation of the good news (the gospel) that was pivotal for the life of the early church.

The Gospel in Acts

- God's promises to Israel are now fulfilled with the coming of Jesus, the Messiah (Acts 2:30; 3:19, 24; 10:43; 26:6–7, 22).
- God anointed Jesus as his Messiah during his baptism (Acts 10:38).
- Jesus began his ministry in Galilee after his baptism (Acts 10:37).
- Jesus, the Messiah, suffered and died on the cross according to God's own plan (Acts 2:23; 3:13–15, 18; 4:11; 10:39; 26:23).
- God raised Jesus from the dead, and Jesus appeared to his disciples (Acts 2:24, 31–32; 3:15, 26; 10:40–41; 17:31; 26:23).

- God exalted Jesus and gave him the name of Lord (Acts 2:25–29, 33–36; 3:13; 10:36).
- God sent the Holy Spirit to create a new community, the church (Acts 1:8; 2:14–18, 38–39; 10:44–47).
- Jesus will come back one day to judge all people and to make all things new (Acts 3:20–21; 10:42; 17:31).
- The good news of Jesus is for all people, urging them to repent and be baptized (Acts 2:21, 38; 3:19; 10:43, 47–48; 17:30; 26:20).

2. Apologetic Purpose

Judaism was a legal religion in the Roman Empire. This meant that Jews were free to practice their religion as they saw fit. At first, Christianity was viewed as a division or sect of Judaism. However, both Judaism and Christianity soon separated from each other. Christians had to show the citizens of the Roman Empire that their religion was not dangerous, but rather a source of blessings for all.

This apologetic purpose of the book of Acts is best seen in its numerous speeches. There are a total of twenty-four speeches in Acts. Here are four key speeches that explain the gospel message and God's plan for the church and, more generally, all humanity.

Areopagus in Athens, Greece

Four Key Speeches in Acts

SPEECH	AUDIENCE	FOCUS
Peter's speech to the disciples in the upper room Acts 1:16–26	Christians	» Fulfillment of God's purpose in Scripture (verses 16, 20). » Activity of the Holy Spirit (verse 16). » Decision to replace Judas (verse 24).
Peter's speech to the crowd in Jerusalem on Pentecost Acts 2:14–39	Jewish not-yet believers	» God's actions as fulfilling his promises in Joel (verses 16–21). » God's actions and acceptance of Jesus' life, death and resurrection (verses 22–24). » God made Jesus Lord and Messiah (verse 36).
Peter's speech to Cornelius's household in Caesarea Acts 10:34–43	Gentile not-yet believers	» God shows no partiality (verse 34). » Jesus' preaching came from God (verse 36). » God anointed Jesus with the Holy Spirit (verse 38). » God raised Jesus from the dead (verse 40). » The apostles are witnesses to these events (verse 41). » God appointed Jesus as judge (verse 42).
Paul's speech at the Areopagus in Athens Acts 17:22–34	Pagans	» God has revealed himself (verse 23). » God is creator and sustainer of the world (verse 24–25). » God is the Lord of all nations (verse 26). » God wants people to seek and find him (verse 27–28). » Idolatry misses the mark (verse 29). » God calls all humanity to repentance (verse 30). » God appointed Jesus as judge by raising him from the dead (verse 31–32).

3. Unifying Purpose

As the church was growing numerically and geographically, the issue of how to include gentiles came to the forefront. This is especially seen in Acts 15 where Luke records how Paul, Peter, and other church leaders gathered in Jerusalem to address how to incorporate gentiles into what was, at that time, mostly a Jewish church.

Although both the gospel of Luke and the book of Acts emphasize the mission to gentiles, the work among Jews was equally important. By focusing the narrative both on the apostle Peter who ministered primarily in Jerusalem and Paul who ventured to spread the gospel to the gentile world, Acts shows the importance of preaching the gospel to everyone.

4. Teaching Purpose

Acts was meant to be a book of instruction for the many new believers throughout the Roman Empire. They needed to know the origin of their faith (gospel of Luke) and the way the power of the gospel spread through the empire (book of Acts). As believers could trace God's actions in the Old Testament, they could also trace the actions of the Holy Spirit in their time. The history of the book of Acts is the history of God's people, and it shows how the Spirit has moved (and still is moving today) throughout the world and in the church.

OUTLINE OF THE BOOK OF ACTS

1. **The work of Jesus continues with the apostles** (1:1–11)
2. **The mission in Jerusalem** (1:12–8:3)
   a. The ministry of Peter (1:12–5:42)
   b. The ministry of Stephen (6:1–8:3)
3. **The mission in Samaria and Judea** (8:4–11:18)
   a. The ministry of Philip (8:4–40)
   b. The conversion of Saul (Paul) (9:1–31)
   c. The ministry of Peter continues (9:32–11:18)
4. **The mission toward the "ends of the earth"** (11:19–28:29)
   a. The ministry of Barnabas (11:19–30)
   b. The conclusion of Peter's ministry (12:1–19a)
   c. The death of Herod Agrippa (12:19b–25)
   d. The ministry of Paul and Barnabas: First missionary journey (13:1–14:28)
   e. The Jerusalem Council (15:1–35)
   f. The ministry of Paul and Silas: Second missionary journey (15:36–18:22)
   g. The ministry of Paul: Third missionary journey (18:23–21:14)
   h. Paul in Jerusalem (21:15–23:22)
   i. Paul in Caesarea (23:23–26:32)
   j. Paul's journey to Rome (27:1–28:29)
5. **Conclusion** (28:30–31)

GOD, JESUS, AND THE HOLY SPIRIT

There are dozens of people named in the book of Acts—and dozens more unnamed. Yet through the lives Paul, Peter, and every person in Acts and behind the scenes of every amazing story is one main character. The focus of this story is God. He is the one who worked through the early church as God the Father, God the Son (Jesus Christ), and God the Holy Spirit.

God: The Center of the Christian Story

The book of Acts tells the story of God in relation to the community of followers of Christ:

- God is the creator (Acts 7:48–50).
- He enables people to be his followers (Acts 2; 4:24–29).
- He is the God of Israel's ancestors (Acts 3:13; 22:14; 24:14).
- He is the God of the gentiles (Acts 10:45; 11:18; 15:7–9, 14; 21:19–20).

In Acts, we encounter the same God of grace and mercy we find in the Old Testament. He has taken the initiative to rescue his people, just as he had promised he would, and he extends the invitation to people of all nations.

Jesus: The Lord of All

We learn about God by knowing his Son, Jesus Christ. As the epistle to the Hebrews teaches, "... in these last days he has spoken to us by his Son" (Heb. 1:2). If the Old Testament reveals God, the New Testament perfects that revelation in the person of Jesus. We learn much about Jesus in the book of Acts.

Jesus is ...

The Promised Messiah	Acts 2:36; 3:20; 5:42; 8:5; 17:3; 18:5
The Son of David	Acts 2:30; 13:23
Lord	Acts 2:36; 10:36

The Son of God	Acts 9:20; 13:33
A Prophet Like Moses	Acts 3:22–23; 7:37
A Servant of the Lord	Acts 3:13, 26; 4:30
The Son of Man	Acts 7:56
The Righteous One	Acts 3:14; 7:52; 22:14
The Author of Life	Acts 3:15
The Prince (Leader) and Savior	Acts 5:31
One Destined to Suffer	Acts 3:18; 17:3; 26:23
One Executed Unjustly	Acts 2:23–24; 3:13–15; 8:32–33; 13:28

The Holy Spirit: The Mover

The Holy Spirit is the one who makes the mission possible. As seen in Acts, the Spirit directs and compels believers to take the gospel to all people and he empowers them to do so. The Spirit is such a force in the story of Acts that some have suggested that the book, rather than being called by its traditional name, *The Acts of the Apostles,* should be called *The Acts of the Holy Spirit.*

From Acts, we learn that:

- The Spirit comes upon Jews and gentiles alike as the sign of God's acceptance (Acts 10:45).
- The indwelling of the Spirit is the common experience of believers (Acts 19:1–6).
- Despite persecution and setbacks on the mission, the Spirit still brings believers joy (Acts 13:52).
- The Spirit moves the mission of God forward (Acts 2:1–41; 4:31; 8:29).

THE CHURCH IN ACTS

Forming the church was God's initiative. It was (and still is) an extension of her Lord. This new community of believers in Acts was characterized by the following six traits.

1. Baptism

The powerful symbolism of baptism shaped the identity of the church. People in this new community were those who died to their old selves and were born again, empowered and sealed by the Holy Spirit. This was a new identity in Christ, where there should no longer be gentile or Jew, or any other social or biological characteristic that segregated them. They were all united as one body.

> When they believed Philip as he proclaimed the good news of the kingdom of God and the name of Jesus Christ, they were baptized, both men and women.
>
> ACTS 8:12

2. Worship

For the church, worship was a visual declaration of their deepest beliefs. In worship, believers expressed with their whole beings what was most important. Praising their Lord was also a humbling experience, where believers recognized their ultimate dependence on God.

> When they heard this, they had no further objections and praised God.
>
> ACTS 11:18

3. Fellowship

The life of the new community of believers was central to their message. This community was characterized by an intimate fellowship with other believers and with the Lord. Fellowship with other believers flows from fellowship with God. In the breaking of bread (which most likely included the Lord's Supper) fellowship became a central part of the Christian community.

> All the believers were one in heart and mind. No one claimed that any of their possessions was their own, but they shared everything they had. With great power the apostles continued to testify to the resurrection of the Lord Jesus. And God's grace was so powerfully at work in them all that there were no needy persons among them.
>
> Acts 4:32–34

> They devoted themselves to the apostles' teaching and to fellowship, to the breaking of bread and to prayer.
>
> ACTS 2:42

4. Teaching

The church was *apostolic* because it was founded on the teachings of the apostles. They taught all that Jesus had taught them and what the Spirit revealed to them.

> With great power the apostles continued to testify to the resurrection of the Lord Jesus. And God's grace was so powerfully at work in them all.
>
> ACTS 4:33

5. Mission

The church's mission was to carry forth God's mission. Through believers' lives and their spoken testimony, God spread his kingdom from Jerusalem outward. The church was (and still is) God's active representative on earth. Just as Jesus suffered for carrying out God the Father's mission, so too, the apostles and first Christians faced persecution and rejection for the mission (Acts 14:22).

> [Paul] witnessed to them from morning till evening, explaining about the kingdom of God, and from the Law of Moses and from the Prophets he tried to persuade them about Jesus.
>
> ACTS 28:23

6. Leadership

Leadership was vital during the early formative years of the church. There are many important leaders in the book of Acts who faced all kinds of challenges: Stephen, James, Barnabas, Silas, Priscilla, Aquila, and, especially Peter and Paul.

> They chose Judas (called Barsabbas) and Silas, men who were leaders among the believers.
>
> ACTS 15:22

BAPTISM IN ACTS

Before his ascension, Christ gave his disciples a command about what do after he left this world: to make disciples and baptize them. This command is known as the Great Commission.

> Therefore go and make disciples of all nations, baptizing them in the name of the Father and of the Son and of the Holy Spirit, and teaching them to obey everything I have commanded you. And surely I am with you always, to the very end of the age.
>
> MATTHEW 28:19–20

The first Christians baptized new believers from all sorts of backgrounds, ethnicities, and social statuses. Here are a few examples from the book of Acts:

- When Peter was speaking to a large crowd during Pentecost, the audience was "cut to the heart" and asked, "What shall we do?" Peter replied, "Repent and be baptized, every one of you, in the name of Jesus Christ for the forgiveness of your sins." About three thousand people accepted Peter's message and were baptized (Acts 2:5–41).

The word *baptize* comes from the Greek verb *baptizo*, meaning to cover or plunge in water, wash, dip, immerse.

- The apostle Philip explained the good news of Jesus to a devout Ethiopian official. When the man believed, he immediately asked to be baptized (Acts 8:26–40).

- Paul (Saul) was a Pharisee who relentlessly persecuted Christians. After an encounter with the risen Lord on the road to Damascus, he believed in Jesus and was later baptized (Acts 9:18).

- When Peter saw that God had poured out the Holy Spirit on Cornelius—a devout, God-fearing Roman centurion—and his household, Peter immediately gave orders that they should be baptized (Acts 10:1–48).

- A businesswoman named Lydia became the first convert in Europe when she heard the apostle Paul's message. She and her household were baptized (Acts 16:11–15).

- After witnessing the power of God through Paul and Silas who were prisoners, their jailer brought them to his house where they explained the message of salvation to everyone present. The jailer and his household believed and were immediately baptized (Acts 16:25–34).

DISCIPLES AND APOSTLES

The word *disciple* means "learner" or "student." In ancient times, a teacher would take one or more followers under his wing in a kind of master-apprentice relationship. The disciple's goal was to become like his mentor—to learn from him, glean his wisdom, and emulate his life. The teacher's goal was to impart important knowledge and skills that the student could eventually pass on to others.

Jesus didn't only instruct his twelve disciples (the idea behind the word *disciple*), he also sent them on missions, the idea behind the word *apostle. Apostle* means "one who is sent," "messenger," or "envoy."

- The *apostle* designation was given by Jesus to the twelve men he handpicked to lead the early church: "[Jesus] called his disciples to him and chose twelve of them, whom he also designated apostles" (Luke 6:13).
- After Judas betrayed Christ and committed suicide, Matthias was chosen to take his place as one of the twelve apostles (Acts 1:15–26).
- Though not one of the twelve apostles, Paul refers to himself several times in his letters as an apostle appointed by Jesus Christ (1 Cor. 1:1; 2 Cor. 1:1; Gal. 1:1), and even, specifically, as an "apostle to the Gentiles" (Rom. 11:13).
- The author of Acts refers to Paul and Barnabas as apostles (Acts 14:14).

CHAPTER 3

The World of the First Christians

The book of Acts takes the reader on a journey. It's a spiritual journey, as believers in Jesus Christ are shaped by the Holy Spirit to form the church, which itself changes and expands throughout the story of Acts. But it's also a geographical journey. Events in Acts begin in the hills of Jerusalem, then move outward to the roads of Asia Minor and the harbors around the Aegean Sea. Each region had its own history and developed its own culture, yet they had one thing in common: they were all controlled by the emperors in Rome.

POLITICAL ATMOSPHERE

The Roman Empire during the time of the New Testament was going through several transitions of leadership. Gaius Octavius, later known as Octavian, consolidated power from the Roman Republic and became the first Roman emperor. (He was the emperor at the time of Jesus' birth.) He added the title "Son of the Divine" to his name to strengthen ties with his adoptive father Julius Caesar, after the Roman Senate declared Julius Caesar a god. Octavian greatly expanded Roman rule all around the Mediterranean Sea.

During the time Jesus was a child living in Nazareth, Tiberius succeeded Octavian. The Roman Empire flourished under Tiberius's reign, but some religious friction began to develop. The Jewish population in Rome grew to have a sizable impact on the citizens of the city. Roman leaders saw Jewish belief in *one* God and their rejection of the many gods of the Roman pantheon (including Caesar!) as undermining the government. Christianity also developed during the last few years of Tiberius's life. In attempts to quell the growing religious friction, Tiberius tried to legalize Christianity. The Roman senate, however, did not agree and made Christianity illegal, saying it undermined the empire.

Caligula succeeded Tiberius, his adoptive grandfather, as emperor in AD 37. He led a complex and cruel life. He reveled in extravagant parties and indulged his sexual fantasies. Wielding unconstrained political power, Caligula became more and more intolerable to be around because of his abrasive personality. In the end, he was killed by his own guards, who then appointed Claudius as ruler in AD 41.

Claudius spent much of his life defending his right to rule. He led several ambitious building campaigns, instituted tax reforms, and focused on strengthening ties with the senate. However, the religious friction that developed under Tiberius's reign did not go away. Claudius saw the Jews as troublemakers who undermined his right to rule, and he expelled them from Rome. Gentile Christians, however, were not expelled from Rome, which amplified the Jewish-gentile animosity in the early Roman church. (This division was addressed by Paul in his letter to the Romans.) Claudius's edict to remove the Jews from Rome forced Priscilla and Aquila to go to Corinth where they eventually met Paul (Acts 18:2).

Religion in the Empire

The Roman Empire was polytheistic (belief in many gods) and normally did not object to people worshiping gods of their choosing. In effect, they absorbed additional gods into the pantheon of Roman gods. The only catch was that all people had to honor the Roman gods too, which was a sign of their honor for Rome.

Jews were in a tricky position because their religion forbade the worship of other gods for any reason. For Jews, there was one God and only one God (Deut. 6:4). They refused to offer sacrifices to Roman gods, actions which Rome considered an affront against its sovereignty. Roman rulers were somewhat tolerant of Jews because they preserved an ancient religion, and Rome was motivated to prevent the Jews in Judea and surrounding areas from revolting—but Rome still kept a close eye on them. When the Jews or the early Jewish Christians gained popularity, Rome was not happy. Both the Jewish and Christian faiths were often viewed as political insubordination to Rome.

Pantheon, the temple to all the gods of Rome. Today the building is the Basilica of St. Mary and the Martyrs.

After Claudius died, Nero became the fifth Roman emperor in AD 54. (This was around the time of Paul's third missionary journey in Acts.) Nero was a young and extravagant ruler who spent as much time developing the cultural life in the empire as he did expanding his networks of trade. Religious animosity continued to grow, and taxation was high, leading to even greater tension. This was the context during the latter part of Acts. When Paul was imprisoned in Caesarea and made his appeal to Caesar, Nero was that Caesar (Acts 25:11).

About five years after the events in Acts, a fire ravaged Rome for more than six days. Nero blamed the Christians for the fire, and as a result, Christians were relentlessly pursued, captured, thrown to beasts, and burned alive. It's believed that both Peter and Paul were executed in these persecutions.

Shortly after the fire in Rome, the heat of religious friction burst into flames around the area of Caesarea, resulting in a Jewish revolt against Rome that spread through the region of the Galilee. Nero sent his military commander, Vespasian, to quell the rebellion. Nero died before the rebellion was ended, and Vespasian inherited the empire. He governed during the time when the Romans destroyed Jerusalem and the temple in AD 70.

ROMAN EMPIRE AT THE TIME OF ACTS

JOURNEY THEME IN LUKE AND ACTS

The book of Acts is geographically detailed from beginning to end. The message of the death and resurrection of Jesus spreads out from Jerusalem into the rest of the Roman Empire. This travel theme is a carryover from the gospel of Luke. Starting in Luke 9 and continuing through chapter 19, Luke details the long and purposeful journey taken by Jesus and the disciples to Jerusalem for the final time. Then the narrative slows down considerably as Luke details the events of Passover week leading up to the crucifixion and resurrection of Jesus.

Acts picks up the narrative where the gospel of Luke leaves off and continues the journey theme, but in reverse order. The gospel moves from Jerusalem outward. The book also shifts the focus of the narratives from Jesus to the Holy Spirit.

- God invades planet earth from the outside in as a baby (Luke 1:5–4:13).
- Jesus invades Galilee of the gentiles first (Luke 4:14–9:50).
- Jesus invades Samaria and Judea (Luke 9:51–19:27).
- Jesus invades Jerusalem at Passover (Luke 19:28–22:46).

CRUCIFIXION, RESURRECTION, and ASCENSION
Luke 22:47–Acts 1:11

- The Spirit takes Jerusalem at Pentecost (Acts 1:12–7:60).
- The Holy Spirit takes Judea and Samaria (Acts 8:1–40).
- The Holy Spirit takes the nations (Acts 9:1–28:31).
- The Holy Spirit takes the world from the inside out through the body of Christ, the church.

Restoration

Both Luke and Acts explore the concept of *restoration* within the journey theme. In Luke, Jesus' role as Messiah prompted his final journey to Jerusalem. Along the way, he challenged his disciples to reform their assumptions of what the Messiah should do. Jesus was in the process of restoring the kingdom of God, but his work was not primarily political, as many people assumed. He would not be like King David, with boundaries marking the edges of a kingdom. Jesus' goal was bigger because his version of restoration included all people. Jesus displayed this throughout his life, when he interacted with rich and poor, men and women, adults and children, farmers and scholars, Jews and gentiles. His actions demonstrated what it meant for the Jewish Messiah to include all people in God's kingdom.

Unlike every human kingdom, God's kingdom has no borders. His kingdom is not evident in human power and prestige, but in the changed lives of the citizens of the kingdom.

Even after following Jesus for many years, the disciples still anticipated the restoration of a human kingdom that looked like King David's. God's vision was bigger. He was restoring all of creation, as Peter explained to a Jewish crowd at the temple:

> Heaven must receive [Jesus Christ] until the time comes for God to restore everything, as he promised long ago through his holy prophets.
>
> ACTS 3:21

At the beginning of Acts, the disciples do not yet realize the full extent of restoration. Jesus instructs them in Acts 1:4–5 to wait in Jerusalem for the gift God would give them—the Holy Spirit. But they ask, "Lord, are you at this time going to restore the kingdom to Israel?" (verse 6). The disciples' hope for the restoration of the kingdom portrays a persistent confusion about the kingdom of God, the restoration of Israel, and the (presumed) national independence (see Luke 22:24–27). Jesus reframed their attention, and told them to wait for the Spirit, and then they would be sent as witnesses "in Jerusalem, and in all Judea and Samaria, and to the ends of the earth" (Acts 1:8). It would take actual journeys to various people groups within different contexts for the disciples to fully understand the extent of the restoration God offered.

Translating the Gospel Story

Within the journey theme is an amazing act of translation. Jewish believers took the story of Jesus, which was so powerful because it was anchored in Israelite and Jewish narratives, and communicated it to a people who did not share their land, scriptures, or history. In the beginning of Acts, the disciples talk with other Jews and use insider language to make convincing points about Jesus. By the end of Acts, Paul speaks to gentiles who do not understand Jewish customs or history and he tries to communicate why a Jewish story is vitally important to them. The expansion of the gospel from Jerusalem and into the Roman world was not a departure from the Israelite story but an invitation for more people to join their story.

Even though Acts follows the expansion theme, the early church was always looking back to Jerusalem and the events that happened there: the life, death, and resurrection of Jesus. This is what anchors the good news that the church took into many different cultural contexts. The Holy Spirit moved and the apostles followed. No physical or ethnic boundary limited the restoration offered by God's kingdom as long as the story of restoration was fully embedded in the events in Jerusalem.

Restoration at Pentecost

The gospels tell us that Jesus was crucified during the festival of Passover which was celebrated in March/April. Passover was the first festival of the Jewish religious calendar when pilgrims congregated at the temple to remember what God did for their ancestors. This festival celebrated the time when God delivered his people out of the hands of Egyptian slavery.

According to the Jewish calendar, the next pilgrim festival was Shavuot which was seven weeks (or forty-nine days) after Passover. This festival remembered the covenant that God made with his people at Mount Sinai—the giving of the Torah (the law of Moses). Exodus 19:16–19 describes God showing up at Sinai with words like *thunder, lightning, loud sounds,* and *fire.* Despite the physical manifestation of God on the mountain, the people down below created a golden calf idol. The consequence of their sin at Sinai was the death of three thousand people (Ex. 32:28). Shavuot reminded the Jews of all those events at Sinai.

Jesus died during the Passover celebration, and Acts 1:3 says that Jesus appeared to the disciples over a period of forty days, teaching about the kingdom of God. For the original readers, they would have understood that these events happened shortly before Shavuot. Acts 2:1 begins this way: "When the day of Pentecost came." The word *Pentecost* comes from the Greek word that means "fiftieth." The day of Pentecost, then, was Shavuot.

Pentecost by Jean II Restout (1732)

On that day, the followers of Jesus were gathered together in one place. Notice how the Holy Spirit appeared to them. The place was engulfed by loud sounds, a cloud, and tongues of fire. The imagery helps readers of Acts make a connection across time. Shavuot reminded the people of the grace of God in giving them the Torah at Mount Sinai, and also the danger of death in turning away from God. Those were also the stories and images that were on the minds of the people who gathered in Jerusalem to celebrate. Now on Pentecost, using similar imagery of loud sounds, wind, and fire, the Holy Spirit showed up to baptize the church into a new covenant (Acts 2:1–4).

The book of Acts then records:

> Now there were staying in Jerusalem God-fearing Jews from every nation under heaven.
>
> ACTS 2:5

Why were so many different people in Jerusalem? For Shavuot! These were God-fearing Jews who lived in different lands but who made the journey to Jerusalem to celebrate this significant holy day at God's temple. The list in Acts 2:9–11 specifies that Jews came from Parthia (eastern lands outside of Rome's control), Asia Minor (modern day Turkey), Egypt and northern Africa, Rome, and islands in the Mediterranean. This is a remarkable list because it tells the history of how far abroad the Jews lived after the Babylonian exile. Readers are reminded again of the diversity of language, place, and cultural views of the Jews. They lived around the Mediterranean Sea and as far east as the Parthian empire. Their geography and their experience with whichever empire ruled them influenced how they practiced Judaism. Yet they were unified despite their differences in traveling to Jerusalem on that significant day to remember how God created a covenant with them as his people.

On Pentecost, pilgrims from these diverse places heard "the wonders of God" spoken in their own language (Acts 2:11). In response to their amazement, Peter stood before the crowds to explain the events of the day. He used Joel 2:28–32 and Psalms 16:8 and 110:1 to explain the mission of Jesus Christ and the important role of the Holy Spirit. Many Jews that day believed and were baptized. In fact, the number baptized was three thousand, the same number of Israelites who had died at the base of Mount Sinai!

THE GOSPEL ACROSS CULTURES

Jesus instructed his followers to wait in Jerusalem for the Spirit; only then would they be sent as witnesses in "Jerusalem, and in all Judea and Samaria, and to the ends of the earth" (Acts 1:8). While these instructions can be understood as an expansion outward in successively larger circles—like ripples from a pebble dropped in a pond—there is also another aspect to consider. Each place named represents not only a geographical location, but a worldview.

Places preserve memories and shape how people understand their world. For first-century Jews, memory of their Israelite history was embedded into the rocks and dirt around them, making place both a teaching tool and a memory trigger. Jesus effectively used his physical locations to communicate with his audience (for example, Luke 21:5–6). In essence, the disciples were tasked with translating who Jesus was into very different cultural contexts of place and history.

Let's examine each location individually, starting with Jerusalem.

HOLY LAND IN THE NEW TESTAMENT

Jerusalem

When we think of places holding onto memories, Jerusalem is a prime example. From the Israelite point of view, Jerusalem was significant for being the City of David and the home of the temple. Jerusalem was the capital of the Israelite kingdom under kings like David and Solomon, and after them, it remained the capital for the southern kingdom of Judah until its destruction in 586 BC.

After the exile, when the Persian Empire permitted the Jews to return to their lands, a small number chose to go to the place that represented home. They went to Jerusalem and rebuilt the city and the temple in the sixth century BC.

In the following centuries, Jerusalem grew to be a large city. For a short time under Hasmonean leadership, the Jews gained independence from foreign rule with Jerusalem as their capital. When the Roman Empire took control, Jerusalem remained the primary seat of local government due to the centrality of the temple for the Jewish people.

When the Holy Spirit came upon believers in Acts 2, the temple was the focal point of the spread of the gospel. Jews from all the surrounding nations made a pilgrimage to the temple to remember the covenant they made with God at the foot of Mount Sinai in the festival of Shavuot (Pentecost). This large, diverse crowd from inside and outside the Roman Empire took Peter's message about the restoration of God's kingdom back home with them. In a way, one could say that Peter's sermon reached the "ends of the earth." However, all the people in the crowd, both Jews and converts to Judaism, shared a similar background. When Peter addressed the crowd, he used Jewish insider language. His sermon was based on knowledge of the Hebrew Scriptures, drawing from passages in the book of Joel and Psalms 16 and 110. Only those familiar with Israelite history and writings would understand Peter's sermon. As long as the message stayed in Jerusalem, it inhabited a Jewish, temple-centric story.

Second Temple

Judea

The bends and folds of the Judean hills created a landscape that discouraged interaction with outsiders. Difficult terrain prohibited easy travel and thus there was less interaction with other cultures and ideas. From the time the Israelites moved into the land to the time they were ruled by Rome, the Judean hills fostered communities that were slow to change.

The conservative nature of Judea was noticeable even in early Roman politics. While establishing his authority and legitimate right to rule, Herod the Great built several palaces in the hill country, including one in Jerusalem. When Herod died in 4 BC, control of Judea passed first to his son Archelaus and then to Roman governors. Those governors quickly moved the primary place of governance out of the temple-centric, Judean hills to the Roman-centric coastal city of Caesarea.

Jews living in Judea did not have the same number of Roman soldiers or caravans of traders passing through their towns. They were often more resistant to Jesus, while the Jews of Galilee, on the other hand, flocked to hear him speak.

As Acts tells the story of the gospel leaving Jerusalem, the message reached the Jews first—and with astonishing success. Acts 5:12–16 says the people from surrounding towns in Judea went to Jerusalem to see what

Judean hills

was happening. News of the events in Jerusalem was spreading, and the communities that had previously resisted Jesus now sought explanations for what they heard.

Jerusalem and Judea had always been anticipated places of restoration. Both locations preserved memories of David's kingdom, so it was assumed that a newly established kingdom of God would certainly be centered there. The disciples spreading the message of restoration to Jerusalem and Judea was not unexpected. But Jewish ideas of restoration would be stretched with the next move into the unexpected land of Samaria.

Samaria

The geography of Samaria was similar to that of Judea and therefore had a similarly strong influence on its inhabitants. However, some valleys in strategic areas created more opportunities for people to be open to outside influences.

The hills of Samaria were saturated with Israelite memories.

- It was the land of Joseph's burial (Josh. 24:32).
- Mounts Ebal and Gerizim were physical reminders of the covenant between God and his people (Deut. 11:29–32; Josh. 8:30–35).
- When the united Israelite kingdom split in two, one of the capital cities was Samaria (1 Kings 16:24).
- The fall of the Northern Kingdom to Assyria was marked by the destruction of the city of Samaria in 722 BC. Soon after, the surrounding geographical region took on the name of Samaria after the fallen capital city.

The Bible records how Assyria replaced the Israelite population with other peoples (2 Kings 17:24). The newcomers embraced a version of the Jewish religion, although they continued to worship their own gods as well (2 Kings 17:25–41). During some religious reforms, several people from the historic northern kingdom reformed their religious practices and even contributed to the refurbishing of the temple (2 Chron. 30:3–11, 18; 34:9). People in the Samarian hill country became known as the Samaritan people. We have little information on the details of their history, but there is evidence that they had their own version of the Pentateuch—the first five books of the Old Testament. They considered themselves to be the true sons of God.

Generations later, conflict sprung up between the Jews who returned to Jerusalem from exile and the people already established in the Samaritan community to the north (see Neh. 4; 6). Each group claimed to be the rightful chosen people of God. The animosity depicted in the books of Ezra and Nehemiah flowered into a deep hostility between the Jews and Samaritans that persisted through Jesus' day.

The geographical regions of Judea and Samaria were considered one political unit by Rome but not by the people who lived there. Their territories held memories of the past that reinforced separation between the populations. Despite such old animosity, Jesus purposefully interacted with the Samaritans (Luke 9:52–54; 10:33–37; 17:11–19). Through his own life and teachings, Jesus demonstrated how the gospel message included the Samaritans as well.

In the book of Acts, when the young Christian community in Jerusalem was persecuted, they fled to the surrounding hills of Judea and Samaria. Philip had great success sharing the gospel in Samaria, prompting other apostles to follow him there (Acts 8:1, 4–25). The movement of the Holy Spirit to the Samaritans was the first clue that the restored kingdom of God included more than the Jews.

Hills of Samaria

The restoration for the Samaritans was surprising, but in some ways they did share the deep-seeded history of the Israelites. Expanding the gospel narrative to the "ends of the earth," however, was a far more foreign context.

The Ends of the Earth

If Acts 1:8 was only a geographical list of names, you would expect Galilee to come after Samaria, especially with so many of Jesus' disciples being from Galilee. But the disciples were told instead to go to the ends of the earth. Where does that begin and what does that mean?

Of all of the place names given in Acts 1:8, the "ends of the earth" is the one that required reaching beyond specific places that held onto layers of Israelite and Jewish history and to going beyond any of the places where the disciples followed Jesus. The use of the phrase "ends of the earth" echoes Isaiah's message that the final restoration will go beyond Judah and Israel:

> I will also make you a light for the Gentiles, that my salvation may reach to the ends of the earth.
>
> ISAIAH 49:6

Maybe Isaiah's message was also on Simeon's mind when he saw the infant Jesus at the temple and recognized God's salvation as "a light for revelation to the Gentiles and the glory of your people Israel" (Luke 2:32).

The book of Acts records the ways the early church struggled with how to take a story grounded in the rocks and soil and scenery of Judea and Galilee and translate it to a people in a place different from their own. After all, God didn't make promises about lands belonging to other nations when he made a covenant with the Israelites. He promised his people a specific land where he would dwell among them. To introduce people from foreign and distant places to their narrative and to make the good news about Jesus relevant to them was quite a challenge. The "ends of the earth" required reaching beyond familiar places and cultures and to *every* nation with *every* language.

THE SPREAD OF CHRISTIANITY
Christianity by AD 100
Christianity by AD 300
Boundary of the Roman Empire
BRITAIN
GERMANY
Colonia
SARMATIA
Atlantic Ocean
Rhine River
GAUL
Mt. Blanc
DACIA
Danube River
Black Sea
ILLYRICUM
Marseille
Sinope
ARMENIA
ITALY
THRACE
Byzantium
SPAIN
Rome
Philippi
Ancyra
Puteoli
Thessalonica
Cordoba
ASIA MINOR
Edessa
GREECE
Ephesus
Tarsus
Cádiz
Iconium
Corinth
Athens
Antioch
Carthage
SICILY
SYRIA
NUMIDIA
CYPRUS
MAURETANIA
CRETE
Damascus
Mediterranean Sea
Jerusalem
Cyrene
Alexandria
City or Town
Mountain
0 100 200 miles
0 200 400 km
TRIPOLITANIA
CYRENAICA
ARABIA
Memphis
EGYPT

JEWS AND GENTILES IN THE EARLY CHURCH

The entire opening of the book of Acts is soaked in Jewish history and culture. Those who saw Jesus ascend to heaven were Jews. They were the first to understand the monumental role Jesus played to restore God's kingdom. The next wave of believers were also Jews. They were the pilgrims in Jerusalem who believed what Peter said. They would return to their scattered places both in and outside of the Roman Empire and tell people at home how Jesus was their Messiah.

Jesus Heals the Bleeding Woman, 4th century Christian art in the Catacomb of Marcellinus and Peter, Rome

The early believers' witness was successful to many Jews and gentiles alike, which created a new question about what to do with the gentiles who believed in Jesus. How were they to be incorporated into what was primarily a Jewish Christian church? This was the issue addressed in Acts 15 in the Jerusalem Council.

The setting and the topic of this church leadership meeting in Jerusalem is more complicated than it appears at first glance. The gathering was set against the backdrop of rising Jewish nationalism and political tension. There were early rumblings of a Jewish revolt against Rome. A small but growing number of Jews living in the traditional ancient Israelite lands wanted independence. Each Roman governor sent to those lands to maintain the empire's interests faced the challenging task of keeping the peace as tension continued to build.

It's important to remember that after the exile when the Israelites were stripped of their land, nation, and king, they spent hundreds of years having internal debates about what made them God's people. How were they set apart from the surrounding peoples? They settled on five basic principles: one God, one temple, circumcision, festivals (including the Sabbath), and one sacred text.

The story of Jesus as Messiah, his teachings, and the power of his death and resurrection were all embedded in Jewish history. How could an outsider begin to understand restoration without understanding the Jewish story first? And yet, Jesus told his disciples that his transformative power was not localized to a city or a nation. God's love for people spread beyond political borders and offered restoration to everyone. Therefore, the good news could not be a nationalistic story.

The question remained of how to welcome gentiles into the community of believers without dismissing the Jewishness of Jesus, his teachings, and the history of God's people. Some Jewish believers thought that gentiles needed to convert to Judaism if they were to appreciate and accept the gospel message (Acts 15:1). Among this group were several Pharisees who highly regarded God's teachings. They came from a tradition that urged people to obey God's instructions with their whole hearts. They were mindful of the biblical law and wanted to honor God by carefully following those instructions. From their perspective, it only made sense that gentiles would become a part of God's family by converting to Judaism first.

But then there were the experiences of Peter and Paul. At the Jerusalem Council, Peter repeated his testimony about Cornelius and his household who accepted Peter's witness. Peter argued that the Holy Spirit fell on them even though they had not been circumcised (meaning they had not converted to Judaism).

> God, who knows the heart, showed that he accepted them by giving the Holy Spirit to them, just as he did to us. He did not discriminate between us and them, for he purified their hearts by faith.
>
> ACTS 15:8–9

Why second-guess what God already did? Why place requirements on the gentiles that God did not place on them first? Peter's claim was supported by Paul and Barnabas who stood up to tell the council about what they saw God do among the gentiles.

Still, answering the question about gentiles in the church required more thought. The leaders turned to Scripture and to their past. James quoted a line from the Greek translation of the prophet Amos that says that when God restores the house of David, the rest of humankind will seek the Lord and bear his name (Amos 9:11–12). Other prophets said similar things. The restoration God promised to his people would extend beyond Israel to all people who recognized God's reign (Isa. 2:2–4; Jer. 12:14–17; Zech. 2:10–11; 8:20–23).

So gentiles were a part of God's plan all along, but what was required of them to be joined with the Jewish believers? Again, the council looked to Scripture. Although many laws in the Old Testament are specifically directed at the Israelite nation, there is recognition that the *ger* (Hebrew for "stranger") would always live among them. What laws applied to them? Leviticus 17:7–10 and 18:26 specifically mention laws that applied to both Israelites and foreigners who lived with them. No one should eat food polluted by idols, engage in sexual immorality, or eat the meat from a strangled animal with its blood.

The council concluded that since the Spirit was poured out on gentiles just as the Spirit was poured out on Jews, God must not require gentiles to become Jewish, and so neither would they. However, they would require that gentiles adhere to the three general laws from Leviticus. In so doing, the gentiles would demonstrate their acceptance of the God of Israel.

Peter and Paul, 4th century catacomb, Rome

TEMPLE, SYNAGOGUE, AND CHURCH

Historically, the focal point for Israel was the temple King Solomon built in Jerusalem. It was God's house, the place where God dwelt among his people in the land he gave them. In 586 BC that temple was destroyed by the Babylonians, and the Israelites were exiled from their land and scattered throughout the Babylonian Empire. We cannot ignore how traumatic that time was. Their identity was built around being God's people in the land of inheritance with God in their midst. What happens when you are a people without a kingdom or a temple?

The Israelites in exile (by that time called Jews) began a new habit of gathering together in small local groups to discuss the Scriptures, and so the synagogue was born. The word *synagogue* refers not strictly to a building but to an assembly of people. These gatherings prioritized worship and the study of Scripture. The synagogue was where Jewish people learned from elders and scholars, became educated, and gained strength as a community.

Even though the Jews rebuilt the temple in Jerusalem, the role of the synagogue remained important. Only one temple for one God existed in one place, but the Jews lived in a variety of places. The local synagogue created a place to reaffirm their sense of identity as God's people in the midst of the larger, more influential non-Jewish society.

The Jerusalem temple and local synagogues feature prominently in the book of Acts. After Pentecost, Jewish believers continued to meet in the temple every day. Peter and John were also there performing miracles and explaining how Jesus fulfilled the role of Messiah. Even during Paul's journeys, he repeatedly went back to the temple in Jerusalem.

Whether in the temple complex or in homes, the first believers met together to discuss how Jesus fulfilled Scripture. In this way, the earliest church communities were like the early synagogues. The infant church was assembled by Jews who did as they always did; they started home fellowships to get together and discuss what they had in common.

When the journey theme in Acts takes the reader outside Jerusalem and away from the temple, the narrative focuses more on synagogues. Throughout Paul's travels, when he entered a new city, he went first to the synagogue and discussed Scripture with the Jewish audiences. Paul did not dismiss synagogue gatherings or Jewish worship, but he did complicate the situation by inviting the gentiles into that community.

> At Iconium Paul and Barnabas went as usual into the Jewish synagogue. There they spoke so effectively that a great number of Jews and Greeks believed.
>
> ACTS 14:1

Both Jews and gentiles in the new Christian community faced challenges about how to live and worship as one church—one body of Christ. The Jews who were scattered throughout different nations used the synagogue as a place to remember their identity as God's people distinct from the culture around them. What would it look like to have Jews next to gentiles in the space where God was worshiped? Gentiles in the Roman world had to readjust their worldview and not only worship the God of the Jews but also reject all other gods. Both Jewish and gentile Christians needed to give up the nationalist desire to have land, government, and control to understand the borderless quality of the kingdom of God.

The resurrection of Jesus and the presence of the Holy Spirit required a new way of understanding the world. Like the prophecy in the Old

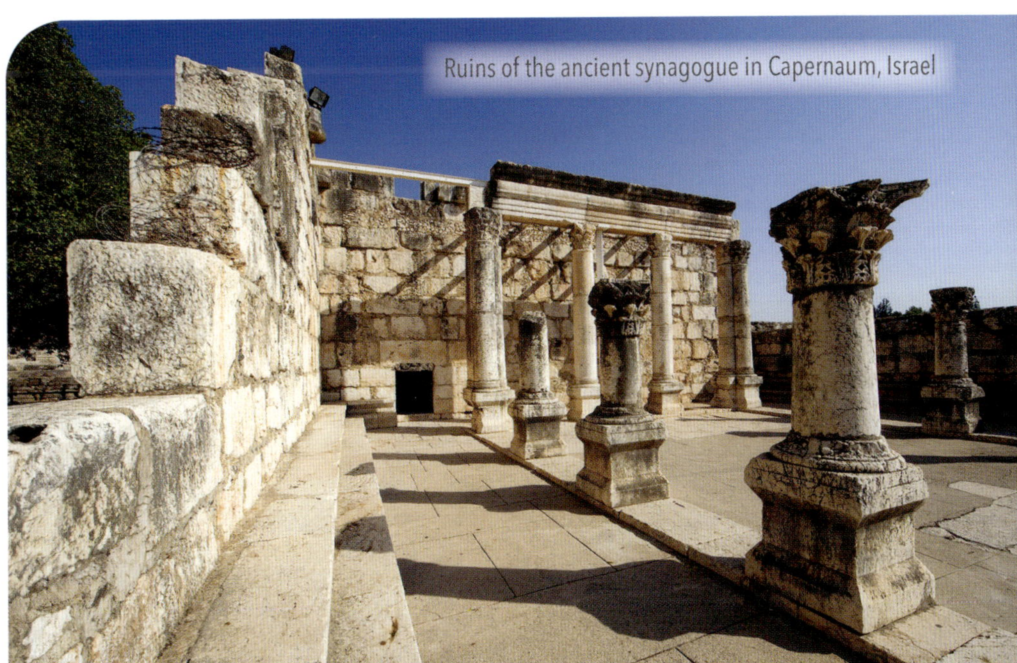

Ruins of the ancient synagogue in Capernaum, Israel

Testament book of Joel that promised a time when all people would be restored (Joel 2:28–32), the resurrection of Christ meant the destruction of barriers between master and servant, men and women, Jew and gentile (Gal. 3:28). All people groups had to figure out how to be one collective church, because the Holy Spirit in Acts made it clear that segregating the church was not an option for God's church.

CHAPTER 4

Life of Paul

As we read through the book of Acts, we discover the fascinating story of Paul, a man who went from being a virulent persecutor of Christians to being repeatedly persecuted as a Christian himself. Paul faced hostile crowds of pagans and devout Jews alike in order to spread the good news of Jesus. He opposed heretics who tried to twist the gospel, as well as disciplined Christians who weren't living up to their faith—sometimes gently, sometimes not so gently. At the same time, Paul was an encouragement to those who worked with and suffered alongside him for the sake of the gospel. Experiencing both hardships and joys, Paul planted churches from Asia Minor to Greece, becoming the early church's greatest missionary.

Saint Paul by Jusepe de Ribera

Paul's story in Acts is not only a historical record of the early church to learn about, but it's a story to be inspired by. God does amazing things through the lives of those who, like Paul, surrender their hard hearts and stubborn wills to God's will and his abundant grace.

THE SETTING

When we first hear of Paul (also called Saul) in the book of Acts, Jesus has risen from the dead and before ascending to heaven has given his disciples a bold mission to be witnesses to the ends of the earth. The disciples received the Holy Spirit at Pentecost and three thousand people were baptized. The church had begun.

At this point in the story, Peter, John, and Stephen are testifying publicly about the good news of Jesus. But not everyone in Jerusalem is pleased with this strange new movement. The city's leaders rile up a crowd, drag Stephen outside the city, and brutally kill him with stones. Enter Saul. The people "laid their coats at the feet of a young man named Saul" (Acts 7:58) as he looked on approvingly at Stephen's execution. Yet he was determined not to remain merely an onlooker.

> Saul began to destroy the church. Going from house to house, he dragged off both men and women and put them in prison.
>
> ACTS 8:3

Saul had plans to completely destroy the church of God. But God had other plans for him.

WHO WAS PAUL?

Paul was born in Tarsus (in modern-day Turkey), probably sometime between AD 2 and 5. Tarsus was a cosmopolitan port city known for its wealth and privilege. Years later, in one of his letters, Paul describes himself as having been "of the people of Israel, of the tribe of Benjamin, a Hebrew of Hebrews" (Phil. 3:5). Although Paul was a Jew, he was also a citizen of the Roman Empire by birth. This dual citizenship would later serve him well in both his life and ministry (Acts 22:25–29; 25:10–12).

While still in his youth, Paul came to Jerusalem where he studied under Gamaliel, the famous Jewish teacher (Acts 22:3; 5:34). Gamaliel was a senior member of the Sanhedrin and may have even been its chief member at one time. He was also a prominent figure among the Pharisees, who were known for their strict observance of both Mosaic and traditional law. The Pharisees were also famous for their hypocrisy, as they often enforced standards that they neglected to keep themselves—something Jesus called them out on regularly (Matt. 6:1–5, 23:1–12; Luke 11:37–52). Nonetheless, Gamaliel had helped save the lives of early Christians. In Acts 4–5, the apostles John and Peter stood trial before the Sanhedrin for preaching the name of Jesus. Gamaliel addressed the Sanhedrin, reminding them of past insurrectionists, then warned the council:

> Leave these men alone! Let them go! For if their purpose or activity is of human origin, it will fail. But if it is from God, you will not be able to stop these men; you will only find yourselves fighting against God.
>
> ACTS 5:38–39

As a result, John and Peter were freed—and "never stopped teaching and proclaiming the good news that Jesus is the Messiah" (Acts 5:42).

Gamaliel's pupil, Paul, however, chose a very different path. Paul became fanatical in defense of his Jewish faith and in stopping the growing Jesus movement. Despite his religious zeal, he was blind to whom Jesus really was—the God he so fervently desired to serve. Paul describes this period of his life saying:

> I persecuted the church of God and tried to destroy it. I was advancing in Judaism beyond many of my own age among my people and was extremely zealous for the traditions of my fathers.
>
> GALATIANS 1:13–14

Paul's religious ambitions against the disciples of Jesus took him beyond Jerusalem, north toward the city of Damascus.

Saul or Paul?

Although other biblical examples of name changes (Abram to Abraham, Jacob to Israel) make it easy to think that Jesus changed Saul's name to Paul on the road to Damascus, the most likely explanation is less dramatic. We read the name Paul for the first time in Acts 13:9 ("Saul, who was also called Paul"). This was more than a decade after the events of Paul's conversion on the Damascus road. It is likely that the dual names, Saul and Paul, were reflective of the apostle's dual heritage as a Hebrew and a Roman: Saul being his Hebrew name and Paul his Roman (or gentile) name. In addition, the first use of the name Paul in Acts occurs in Cyprus, where he leads the Roman proconsul Sergius Paulus to Christ (Acts 13:7–12). As it became increasingly obvious that Paul's mission was to the gentiles, he would use his gentile name more frequently as he traveled further into that world.

JOURNEY TO DAMASCUS

Although the church in Damascus certainly had been formed by the time Paul traveled to the city, there is reason to believe that there were believers there even while Jesus was still on earth. As the capital of Syria and the oldest inhabited city in the world—and given its proximity to Jerusalem, about 130 miles (209 km) to the northeast—it's not surprising that the city of Damascus would be an early stronghold for the church. It would also not be a huge surprise that after persecuting the church in Jerusalem, Paul would set his sights next on Damascus. Some Christians in Jerusalem had fled to Damascus to escape persecution. Paul was heading to Damascus to bring back those refugees to face punishment.

Paul set out for Damascus to apprehend followers of Jesus, but on the way, it was he who was "apprehended by Christ Jesus" (Phil. 3:12 KJV). A great light flashed from heaven, Paul fell to the ground, and the risen Jesus revealed the truth to Paul:

> I am Jesus, whom you are persecuting.
>
> ACTS 9:5

Physically blinded by the experience, Paul arrived in Damascus where the Lord directed a Christian named Ananias to go to Paul and restore his sight. While Paul's physical sight was restored, it was really his spiritual sight that made all the difference. Paul would go on to become a force that influenced the world for God as a disciple of Jesus.

Years later, he would look back and write this about both his old life and his new life:

> In regard to the law, [I was] a Pharisee; as for zeal, persecuting the church; as for righteousness based on the law, faultless. But whatever were gains to me I now consider loss for the sake of Christ.
>
> PHILIPPIANS 3:5–7

Paul Before and After His Encounter with Jesus

BEFORE	AFTER
Approved of the murder of a Christian man named Stephen (Acts 8:1).	Accepted the help of a Christian man named Ananias (Acts 9:17).
"Breathed out murderous threats against the Lord's disciples" (Acts 9:1).	Preached "that Jesus is the Son of God" (Acts 9:20).
Sought out synagogues to get approval, so he could persecute followers of Jesus (Acts 9:1–2).	Went to the synagogues to prove "that Jesus is the Messiah" (Acts 9:20, 22).

PAUL'S "LOST" YEARS

Nearly ten years passed between Paul's encounter with Jesus on the road to Damascus and the start of Paul's first formal missionary journey. The book of Acts is silent about much of this time, but we do gain some insight into this "lost" period from Paul's letter to the Galatians.

Based on this letter, it would appear that Paul did not go to Jerusalem immediately after escaping a plot against his life in Damascus (Acts 9:23–26). In fact, three years would pass. Paul first went to Arabia, then returned to Damascus (Gal. 1:15–18). It is likely that Paul preached in Arabia as well, even though King Aretas IV of Nabatæan (northern) Arabia had been part of the conspiracy to seize Paul in Damascus (2 Cor. 11:32–33). Aretas's actions were probably motivated by the fact that he was the father-in-law of Herod Antipas, who governed Galilee during Jesus' time and whose death is graphically portrayed in Acts 12:20–23.

After Paul's time in Arabia and Damascus, he went to Jerusalem. But he was not yet fully trusted by the leaders of the church:

> When he came to Jerusalem, he tried to join the disciples, but they were all afraid of him, not believing that he really was a disciple.
>
> ACTS 9:26

It is at this point that Barnabas becomes a major figure in the book of Acts. We were introduced to him in Acts 4:36 as Joseph, nicknamed Barnabas (or "son of encouragement"), a Levite from Cyprus. Barnabas had sold a field and laid the money "at the apostles' feet" (Acts 4:37) so that the funds could be distributed among the poor. In Acts 9, he stood up for Paul, recounting all that had happened to Paul on the road to Damascus and "how at Damascus [Paul] had preached fearlessly in the name of Jesus" (Acts 9:27). With Barnabas advocating for him, Paul was finally accepted. Sometime during this period, Paul stayed with the apostle Peter for fifteen days, also meeting with Jesus' brother James (Gal. 1:18–19).

Paul went on to preach in Jerusalem, and once again, he received death threats and was forced to escape, first to Caesarea and ultimately to his hometown of Tarsus (Acts 9:28–30). At this point, the biblical account of Paul's life goes silent for several years. All we know about this time comes from Paul's letter to the Galatians where he wrote that the apostles only heard the report:

> The man who formerly persecuted us is now preaching the faith he once tried to destroy.
>
> GALATIANS 1:23

The account of Paul's life picks up again in Acts 11 after men from Cyprus and Cyrene preached to the gentiles in Antioch of Syria, and, as a result, "a great number of people believed and turned to the Lord" (Acts 11:21). The Jerusalem church sent Barnabas to Antioch. Barnabas, in turn, fetched Paul from Tarsus and "for a whole year Barnabas and Saul met with the church and taught great numbers of people" (Acts 11:26).

During this time, a great famine was predicted in Jerusalem. The church in Antioch determined to send relief. The other believers apparently trusted Barnabas and Paul immensely because they gave them the responsibility of delivering the funds they had collected for those in need in Jerusalem. It is this "service" (or "mission") that is referred to in Acts 12:25.

PAUL'S EARLY TRAVELS

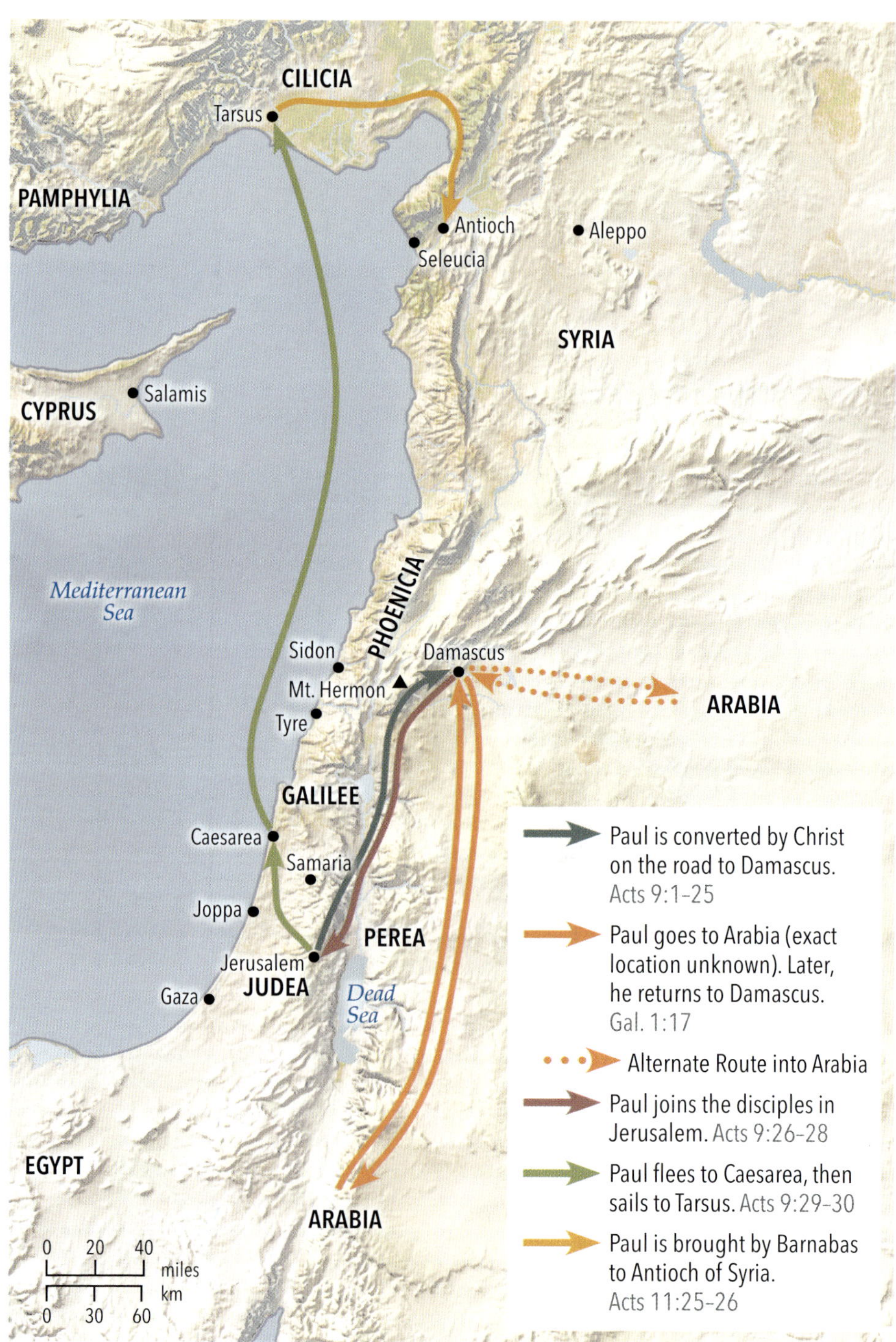

PAUL'S MISSION

Paul had a divine calling. His own goal had been to put an end to the gospel of Jesus, but his mission from God was to spread the gospel to the world. In Galatians, Paul reminds believers:

> Even before I was born, God chose me and called me by his marvelous grace. Then it pleased him to reveal his Son to me so that I would proclaim the Good News about Jesus to the Gentiles.
>
> GALATIANS 1:15–16 NLT

In Antioch of Syria, the Holy Spirit was moving in the prophets and teachers of the church, telling them to "set apart" Paul and Barnabas for special missionary work (Acts 13:1–3). And that they did.

Launching from Antioch, Paul's initial stop on his first formal missionary journey was the island of Cyprus, where he visited two places: Salamis and Paphos. In the city of Salamis, Paul and Barnabas began preaching in the synagogues, as was Paul's custom, especially since there were very few established churches early in his ministry. In contrast to later accounts in Acts, there is no mention of anyone responding to Paul's message—possibly because no one did.

Paphos Archaeological Park, Cyprus

Upon arrival in Paphos, they encountered a sorcerer named Bar-Jesus (or Elymas) who was an advisor to the governor Sergius Paulus. Given the governor's response later in chapter 13 and the fact that the sorcerer was Jewish, it may well have been that the governor already had some interest in the Hebrew Scriptures. But instead of blinding the governor to the faith as the governor's sorcerer had intended (Acts 13:8), the sorcerer himself was blinded when Paul pronounced judgment upon him. As a result, the governor's own spiritual blindness was lifted, and he believed in the Lord.

When Paul arrived in Antioch of Pisidia, he again started by preaching in the synagogue. This time a response is mentioned, and it would become a familiar pattern for Paul and those with him: both Jews and especially gentiles would believe in Christ, but some Jews (often those in leadership) would stir up persecution. These persecutors in Antioch succeeded in driving out Paul and Barnabas, but the apostles were unfazed:

> They shook the dust off their feet as a warning to them and went to Iconium.
>
> ACTS 13:51

This pattern we see throughout Paul's missionary journeys:

- Some people believe the gospel message.
- Some dismiss or ignore it.
- Some outright oppose it.

But Paul's mission—as is all believers' mission—was to testify about the good news of Jesus Christ. Whether or not the people's spiritual blindness was lifted was up to God. As Paul would write many years later to a young pastor named Timothy:

> Do not be ashamed of the testimony about our Lord or of me his prisoner. Rather, join with me in suffering for the gospel, by the power of God. He has saved us and called us to a holy life—not because of anything we have done but because of his own purpose and grace.
>
> 2 TIMOTHY 1:8–9

PAUL'S FIRST MISSIONARY JOURNEY

Travelers: Paul, Barnabas, John Mark
Distance: 1,400 miles (2,300 km)
Dates: AD 47–49

- **Antioch of Syria:** The Holy Spirit sends Paul and Barnabas to be missionaries. John Mark goes along as their helper. Acts 13:1–4

- **Paphos:** Paul confronts a sorcerer and blinds him. Acts 13:5–12

- **Perga:** John Mark leaves the group and returns to Jerusalem. Acts 13:13

- **Antioch of Pisidia:** Paul preaches his longest recorded sermon, and many become believers. Jewish leaders drive Paul and Barnabas out of the city and the Lord calls Paul to focus his ministry on gentiles. Acts 13:14–52

- **Iconium:** A plot to stone Paul and Barnabas forces them to flee the city. Acts 14:1–7

Dates and distances for all Paul's journeys are approximate; travel routes may vary.

- **Lystra:** When Paul heals a lame man, the townspeople think he and Barnabas are Greek gods. Jews from Antioch and Iconium stir up the crowd, and Paul is stoned and left for dead outside the city. But he survives and goes back into the city. Acts 14:8–20
- **Derbe:** Many disciples are added to the church. Acts 14:20–21
- **Derbe to Antioch of Syria:** On the return trip, Paul and Barnabas appoint elders in the churches they had planted. Acts 14:21–25
- **Antioch of Syria:** Paul and Barnabas report·all that God had done. Acts 14:26–28

Antioch of Pisidia

Paul and his companions traveled along the Via Sebaste road that took them up more than 3,600 feet to Antioch of Pisidia (not to be confused with the Antioch in Syria which was Paul's home base). Antioch was on an elevated central basin of Asia Minor. It was an important political hub for Rome, and it flourished economically from the trade routes that converged at this city. In honor of the emperor who poured so much money into the city, the citizens built a temple to Augustus in the heart of the city.

Ruins at Antioch of Pisidia, Turkey

JERUSALEM COUNCIL

At this point in Acts, Paul has concluded his first missionary journey where it began—Antioch of Syria. Here, Paul and Barnabas reported to believers the wonderful news from their journey of how God "had opened a door of faith to the Gentiles" (Acts 14:27). This influx of gentile Christians into newly growing churches—which had been largely composed of Jewish Christians—created a "sharp dispute" (Acts 15:2). This dispute required everyone involved to come to a peaceful resolution and still stay true to Jesus in the process.

As we have already seen in Acts, Paul faced considerable opposition from unbelieving Jews early in his ministry. However, the next phase of Paul's ministry would introduce a new twist: opposition from Christian Jews. Near the end of Paul's first missionary journey, a group known as the Judaizers heavily infiltrated the churches that Paul had just established in the province of Galatia and they started to change church doctrine. These Judaizers were professed Christians who nonetheless insisted that other Christians follow the laws of Judaism. They insisted that circumcision and observance of Mosaic law were essential for salvation. They tried to impose their regulations on gentile converts as well as Jewish ones. The Judaizers' doctrine contradicted everything Paul had been preaching to the Galatians about their newfound freedom in Christ. It suggested that Christ's sacrifice on the cross was not enough—and Paul wanted nothing to do with that!

He wrote the very first of his epistles in the Bible to the Galatians, making his case clear: "We … know that a person is not justified by the works of the law, but by faith in Jesus Christ" (Gal. 2:15–16). This letter shows Paul at his angriest. He had just finished planting these young churches and establishing leadership there, only to see others try to corrupt and destroy them.

> I am astonished that you are so quickly deserting the one who called you to live in the grace of Christ and are turning to a different gospel—which is really no gospel at all. Evidently some people are throwing you into confusion and are trying to pervert the gospel of Christ. But even if we or an angel from heaven should preach a

> gospel other than the one we preached to you, let them be under God's curse!
>
> GALATIANS 1:6–8

In fact, to emphasize the passion of his message, Paul took the pen from his scribe and wrote the end of the letter himself, in large letters (Gal. 6:11).

Paul and Barnabas were appointed to go to Jerusalem to meet with the apostles and elders to resolve this issue. This meeting has come to be known as the Jerusalem Council. The important matter at this point was to uphold the freedom from sin and the salvation that Christ had provided, while, at the same time, maintaining unity within the church. After much discussion, the apostle Peter declared about the Judaizers, "Why do you try to test God by putting on the necks of Gentiles a yoke that neither we nor our ancestors have been able to bear?" (Acts 15:10).

Paul at the Council of Jerusalem

The council had come to a decision. The resolution, first declared by James, was "that we should not make it difficult for the Gentiles who are turning to God. Instead, we should write to them, telling them to abstain from food polluted by idols, from sexual immorality, from the meat of strangled animals and from blood" (Acts 15:19–20). The bottom line, for Jewish and gentile believers alike, was that freedom in Christ meant living in Christ, and that meant avoiding all things and behaviors that honored other gods, for that would have dishonored the one true God. Paul would make this same point years later, in his letter to the Romans:

> What then? Shall we sin because we are not under the law but under grace? By no means! ... But thanks be to God that, though you used to be slaves to sin, you have come to obey from your heart the pattern of teaching

that has now claimed your allegiance. You have been set free from sin and have become slaves to righteousness.

ROMANS 6:15–18

Though the Jerusalem Council helped make clear for believers what freedom and living in Christ really meant, the Judaizers would continue to oppose Paul's mission.

Antioch of Syria

Due to the persecution in Jerusalem, many early believers fled the city and "traveled as far as Phoenicia, Cyprus and Antioch, spreading the word only among the Jews" (Acts 11:19). Others, however, went to Antioch of Syria and started sharing the gospel among the gentiles. From its early days, the church in Antioch was a mixed church of Jews and gentiles alike.

Antioch was also Paul's home base. The city had a more strategic position than Jerusalem. Land routes from the north, east, and south funneled through Antioch and found easy connections with the sea. Rome understood the significance of these routes and protected them by financing extensive building projects there. Antioch ultimately became one of the largest cities in the Roman empire.

Roman road connecting Antioch and Chalcis

PAUL SECOND AND THIRD MISSIONARY JOURNEYS

Paul's second missionary journey took him much farther than his first. After a disagreement with Barnabas about whether John Mark should join them, Paul set off on his second missionary journey, this time accompanied by Silas. Paul and Silas headed to Asia Minor, traveling north overland to revisit churches in Asia Minor, a land route that included an over 6,800 foot incline to arrive in Derbe. Then they set out for Macedonia and then on to Greece. Notable on this trip was Paul's famous Mars Hill sermon to the philosophers in Athens, Greece, where he preached:

> People of Athens! I see that in every way you are very religious. For as I walked around and looked carefully at your objects of worship, I even found an altar with this inscription: TO AN UNKNOWN GOD. So you are ignorant of the very thing you worship—and this is what I am going to proclaim to you.
>
> ACTS 17:22–23

Shaping his message to a particular crowd, Paul preached the good news of Christ's resurrection. This caused some of the elite to sneer, but others became believers. Little by little, wherever Paul went, the church grew.

View of Athens from Mars Hill

PAUL'S SECOND MISSIONARY JOURNEY

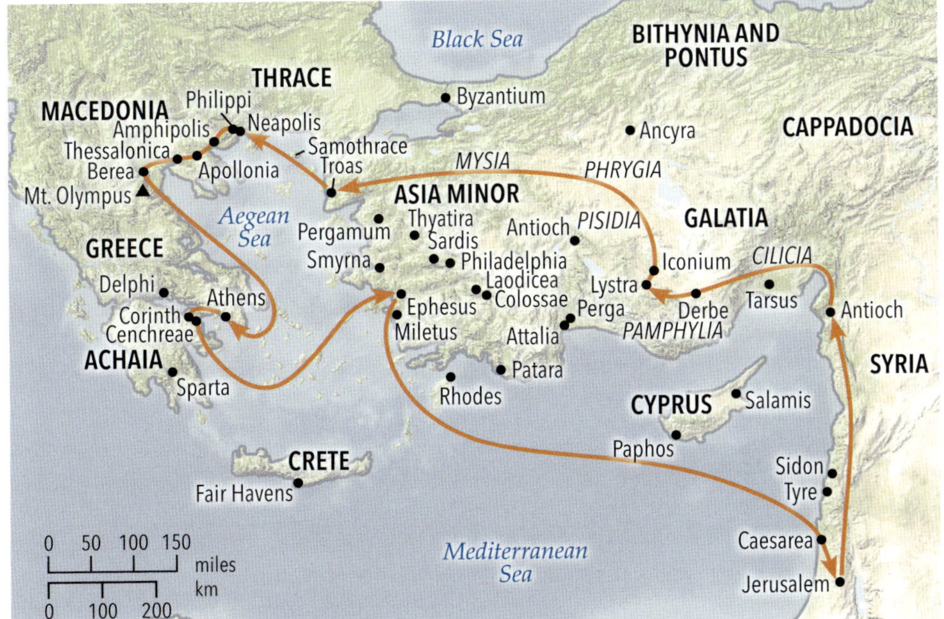

Travelers: Paul, Silas, Timothy, Luke, Priscilla, and Aquila
Distance: 2,800 miles (4,500 km)
Dates: AD 49–51

- **Antioch of Syria:** Paul and Barnabas disagree about who should go with them. Barnabas takes John Mark with him to Cyprus. Paul takes Silas. Acts 15:36–40

- **Cilicia:** Paul and Silas deliver a letter from the Jerusalem church. Acts 15:41 (Acts 15:22–29)

- **Lystra:** Timothy joins them. Acts 16:1–7

- **Troas:** Paul goes to Macedonia after receiving a vision of a man from there. Acts 16:8–10

- **Philippi:** Lydia becomes a Christian. When a fortune-telling slave girl also becomes a Christian, her owners riot. Paul and Silas are thrown in jail. The jailer also becomes a believer. Acts 16:11–40

- **Thessalonica:** A mob in Thessalonica tries to have Paul and Silas arrested. Acts 17:1–9
- **Berea:** Silas and Timothy stay in Berea while Paul goes on. Acts 17:10–15
- **Athens:** Paul sees an altar to an unknown god and preaches to the philosophers at the Areopagus (Mars Hill). Acts 17:16–34
- **Corinth:** Silas and Timothy rejoin Paul. He meets Priscilla and Aquila, who also join him. Acts 18:1–17
- **Cenchreae:** Paul gets his hair cut because he had taken a vow. Acts 18:18
- **Ephesus:** Paul establishes a church, leaving Priscilla and Aquila to tend to it. Acts 18:19–21
- **Antioch of Syria:** Paul returns to his home base of Antioch by way of Jerusalem. Acts 18:22

Not long after the conclusion of Paul's second journey, he went out again, traveling through similar regions as his second journey, revisiting sprouting churches he had planted earlier. On this trip, Paul spent about two years strengthening a church in one very important city, the city of Ephesus.

Ephesus was one of the largest cities in the Roman Empire and one of the most significant port cities of the Aegean Sea. Its temple for the goddess Artemis (Diana)—about 425 feet long, 200 feet wide, 60 feet high (129 x 61 x 18 meters), and supported by 127 columns—was one of the seven wonders of the ancient world. This harbor city had a booming tourist industry, with craftsmen creating souvenirs of Artemis for visitors to take home with them. Ephesus was a pilgrimage site, as well as a major banking center in Asia Minor. It was also known to be a city steeped in superstition and occult practices. By the time Paul arrived in Ephesus, the city was already more dependent on the religious tourist trade than on harbor traffic, as the harbor had begun filling with silt.

Paul preached the gospel initially in the Ephesian synagogues and then in the public lecture halls. God did great miracles through Paul in Ephesus "so that even handkerchiefs and aprons that had touched him were taken to the sick, and their illnesses were cured and the evil spirits left them" (Acts 19:12). These handkerchiefs and aprons were likely used by Ephesian craftsmen who had come to believe in Christ. Because of this explosion of the miraculous, some wandering Jewish exorcists claiming to be able to cast out evil spirits saw a business opportunity. Among them were the seven sons of the so-called "high priest" Sceva who tried to change their business model by casting out evil spirits in Jesus' name. In using the name of Jesus like a magic word, they failed miserably against a demon. They were, in fact, overpowered by the evil spirit, and they "ran out of that house naked and bleeding" (Acts 19:16). But God has a way of taking human attempts at perverting the gospel and making them a catalyst for spreading the real gospel even further. News of this episode shocked the Ephesians. Many "who had practiced sorcery brought their scrolls together and burned them publicly. When they calculated the value of the scrolls, the total came to fifty thousand drachmas" (Acts 19:19). (One drachma was a coin worth about one day's wage.) These scrolls were probably made of papyrus or parchment, so their high value likely had little to do with the quality of their construction but with their supposed magical content. Salvation in Christ was far more valuable to these new Ephesian converts than their "magic" scrolls.

Ruins of the Temple of Artemis near Ephesus

The rapid growth of Christianity in Ephesus proved to be a serious problem to the city's silversmiths who were dependent on the religious tourist trade generated by the temple of Artemis. The power of the gospel not only was changing the religious identity of Ephesus, but it also was bad for business—and so, a riot ensued. It became clear that it was time for Paul to leave the city in which he had invested so much time.

PAUL'S THIRD MISSIONARY JOURNEY

Travelers: Paul, Timothy, Luke, and others
Distance: 2,700 miles (4,300 km)
Dates: AD 52–57

- **Galatia and Phrygia:** Paul visits churches in this region. Acts 18:23
- **Ephesus:** Paul stays in Ephesus two years. So many people convert to Christianity that the silversmiths who manufacture idols start a riot. Acts 19:1–41
- **Macedonia and Greece:** Paul gives encouraging words to believers in this region. He stays three months. Acts 20:1–3
- **Troas:** While Paul is preaching, a young man falls asleep, and falls from a third-story window and dies. Paul revives him. Acts 20:4–12
- **Miletus:** Elders from Ephesus meet the ship at Miletus and Paul tells them that he expects to be imprisoned in Jerusalem. Acts 20:13–38
- **Tyre:** Believers warn Paul not to go to Jerusalem. Acts 21:1–6

- **Caesarea:** A prophet predicts that Paul will be imprisoned and handed over to the gentiles. Acts 21:7–16

- **Jerusalem:** Paul and his team report to the church leaders, who urge Paul to participate in a purification ritual at the temple to counteract rumors that Christianity is anti-Jewish. Acts 21:17–26

PAUL IN JERUSALEM

Doing the right thing can be difficult, especially when all your well-meaning friends are telling you not to do it. This was the situation Paul faced when he resolved to go to Jerusalem. With a farewell address to the elders of the church in Ephesus, Paul headed toward Jerusalem, "not knowing what [would] happen to [him] there" (Acts 20:22). Nevertheless, the Holy Spirit had compelled him to go. How could he deny the Spirit's leading? He couldn't. In fact, he was determined to "finish the race and complete the task the Lord Jesus [had] given [him]" (Acts 20:24).

As Paul completed his third missionary journey—and much like Jesus prior to his death as he "resolutely set out for Jerusalem" (Luke 9:51)—Paul was repeatedly warned by prophets and other disciples of the dangers that awaited him. While in Tyre on his way to Jerusalem, Paul and his entourage (including Luke, the author of the book of Acts) sought out the disciples there and stayed for seven days.

> Through the Spirit [the disciples] urged Paul not to go on to Jerusalem.
>
> ACTS 21:4

This brings up an interesting question: Was Paul disobeying the Spirit by continuing to Jerusalem? The short answer is no. In Acts 20, the Spirit had already told Paul to go to Jerusalem:

> Compelled by the Spirit, I am going to Jerusalem, not knowing what will happen to me there. I only know that in every city the Holy Spirit warns me that prison and hardships are facing me.
>
> ACTS 20:22–23

Though Paul didn't know exactly what would happen to him in Jerusalem, he understood that captivity and persecution were awaiting him. It is likely that when the Spirit had confirmed this to the disciples, they had responded much as Peter first did when Jesus had told his disciples that he was going to Jerusalem to be killed (Matt. 16:21–23). Their response was out of fear and concern for their leader rather than out of faith in God's sovereignty in the matter.

In Caesarea, Paul stayed with Philip, "one of the Seven" who had, years before, been chosen to oversee a food distribution ministry in Jerusalem (Acts 6:1–6; 21:8). It's worth remembering that Stephen, whose stoning Paul had once approved of, was also one of the seven (Acts 8:1). Philip, it appears, had forgiven Paul for his role in Stephen's murder. Also at Caesarea, the prophet Agabus predicted Paul's arrest and imprisonment, and again, the disciples—including Luke, it would appear—begged Paul not to continue. But Paul answered:

> Why are you weeping and breaking my heart? I am ready not only to be bound, but also to die in Jerusalem for the name of the Lord Jesus." When he would not be dissuaded, we gave up and said, "The Lord's will be done."
>
> ACTS 21:13–14

Paul was far less concerned about the dangers and suffering he would face and far more concerned with following Jesus, no matter what the cost.

Upon arriving in Jerusalem, Paul was welcomed by the brothers and then by James and the elders (Acts 21:17–18). About eight years had passed since Paul's visit to Jerusalem when the Jerusalem Council was held. In that time, God had used Paul greatly among the gentiles, and when Paul shared with the church in Jerusalem about all that God had done, "they praised God" (Acts 21:20).

Near the end of his voluntary purification, Paul again entered the temple at Jerusalem. Upon seeing Paul, "Jews from Asia . . . stirred up the whole crowd and seized him" and accused him of bringing Trophimus the Ephesian, one of his traveling companions, into the temple with him

(Acts 21:27–29). Such an accusation flew in the face of the purification Paul had been willing to undergo for the sake of his fellow Jews, but clearly the crowd was willing to believe this slander against Paul.

Paul was dragged out of the temple. The mob beat him until the Roman army arrived and put Paul in chains. Paul had to be physically carried away by the soldiers "because of the violence of the mob" (Acts 21:35). Before he was brought into the barracks, however, he asked to speak to the crowd. It was no small miracle that at this point the crowd all became silent. Standing before his own persecutors, Paul shared his testimony with the hostile audience. He too had once been a persecutor of Christians in Jerusalem before his encounter with Christ. He even mentioned his own role in the death of Stephen, before making a statement (just like Stephen had) that pushed the hostile audience over the edge: "The Lord said to me, 'Go; I will send you far away to the Gentiles'" (Acts 22:21). At this, they began "shouting and throwing off their cloaks and flinging dust into the air, [so] the commander ordered that Paul be taken into the barracks. He directed that he be flogged and interrogated" (Acts 22:23–24). Instead, Paul declared his Roman citizenship to the centurion and asked, "Is it legal for you to flog a Roman citizen who hasn't even been found guilty?" (Acts 22:25). The answer was obviously no. His interrogators stopped.

Paul's Arrest, basilica of Saint Paul

Yet the hardships Paul faced didn't stop. Paul stood trial before the Sanhedrin and then Felix the governor. But Paul's message about "righteousness, self-control and the judgment to come" made Felix afraid, so he had Paul sent to prison (Acts 24:25).

Parallels between Jesus' and Paul's Final Entries into Jerusalem

JESUS	PAUL
Jesus determined to go to Jerusalem, despite the dangers he knew awaited him (Luke 9:51; 13:33).	Paul was compelled by the Spirit to go to Jerusalem, despite the dangers he knew awaited him (Acts 19:21; 20:22-23; 21:8-14).
Jesus arrived in Jerusalem, was welcomed by large crowds, and went to the temple soon afterward (Luke 19:28–48). Jesus was arrested by a Jewish mob, then turned over to the Roman governor for trial (Luke 22:47–54; 23:1-25).	Paul arrived in Jerusalem, was welcomed by the disciples there, and went to the temple soon afterward (Acts 21:17-26). Paul was seized by a Jewish mob that wanted him killed, and later stood trial before Roman governors (Acts 21:30-36; 23:23-26).
During questioning, one of the high priest's officers struck Jesus in the face (John 18:22-23).	The high priest ordered those nearby to strike Paul on the mouth (Acts 23:2–5).
Jesus was questioned by Sadducees, who did not believe in the resurrection (Luke 20:27–38).	Paul pitted the Pharisees against the Sadducees regarding the resurrection (Acts 23:6-9).
At the Last Supper, Jesus took bread, blessed it, broke it, and gave it to the disciples to eat (Matt. 26:26–28; Luke 22:15-20).	On his way to Rome, Paul took bread, gave thanks, broke it, and ate it (Acts 27:35).

Shortly after Paul's arrest in Jerusalem, the Lord appeared to him and said, "Take courage! As you have testified about me in Jerusalem, so you must also testify in Rome" (Acts 23:11). Waiting in prison in Caesarea for two years, Paul knew that his story would not end there; he would go to Rome.

When the new governor, Festus, arrived in Caesarea, Paul did something surprising: he appealed his case to Caesar. To which Festus replied, "To Caesar you will go!" (Acts 25:12). This began Paul's long voyage journey to Rome in which he and his fellow passengers survived a harrowing storm, being lost at sea, and finally shipwrecked on the island of Malta.

Paul did eventually arrive in Rome as he had desired and as the Lord had revealed to him, but he arrived in chains. He remained for two years in Rome under guarded house arrest.

Paul's Larger Mission

A curious question arises about the incident in Acts 21:20–26. Why did Paul, who had been preaching freedom in Christ, choose to go through the Jewish religious rites of purification in Jerusalem?

It's worth noting that this wasn't the first time Paul had done (or requested) something like this. We saw that at Cenchreae Paul had cut his hair because he was under a vow (Acts 18:18)—generally believed to be the vow of a Nazarite, a voluntary vow of separation to the Lord (Num. 6:1–21). Even more radically, Paul had the gentile Timothy circumcised shortly after the Jerusalem Council, "because of the Jews who lived in that area, for they all knew that [Timothy's] father was a Greek" (Acts 16:3).

On the surface, these incidents seem out of line with what Paul taught. However, they line up perfectly with his larger mission. Paul would not have wanted to go out of his way to offend his fellow Jews, even as he clearly preached to them that such rites were in no way necessary for salvation. The clearest rationale for these actions can be seen in Paul's first letter to the Corinthians, written shortly before his arrival in Jerusalem: "Though I am free and belong to no one, I have made myself a slave to everyone, to win as many as possible. To the Jews I became like a Jew, to win the Jews. To those under the law I became like one under the law (though I myself am not under the law), so as to win those under the law. ... I do all this for the sake of the gospel, that I may share in its blessings" (1 Cor. 9:19–23).

PAUL'S JOURNEY TO ROME

Travelers: Paul, Roman guards, Luke, and others
Distance: 2,200 miles (3,500 km)
Dates: AD 59–60

- **Jerusalem:** After Paul is arrested, the Roman commander learns of a death threat against Paul, so he orders an armed escort to take Paul to Caesarea. Acts 23:12–35

- **Caesarea:** Paul is tried before governor Felix, but Felix leaves him in prison for two years. Paul again stands trial, but this time before Festus, the new governor. Paul demands his right as a Roman citizen and appeals his case to Caesar. Herod Agrippa II visits Festus, and Paul appears before him as well. It's decided that Paul should go to Rome. Acts 24:1–26:32

- **Sidon:** The centurion in charge of Paul lets him visit with friends. Then Paul boards a ship and begins his journey to Rome. Acts 27:1–4

- **Crete:** Paul recommends that the ship stay in safe harbor, but the centurion orders the ship to sail on. Acts 27:5–12

- **Malta:** After a two-week storm, the ship is wrecked near the island of Malta. Everyone on the ship makes it to shore. After three months, they set sail again. Acts 27:13–28:11
- **Puteoli:** Paul stays with believers for a week. Acts 28:12–14
- **Forum of Appius and Three Taverns:** Paul is met by believers from Rome. Acts 28:15
- **Rome:** Paul remains under house arrest for two years, sharing the gospel with everyone he can. Acts 28:16–31

Port Cities

Although Paul crosses the interior of Asia Minor (modern day Turkey) four times in the book of Acts, the author gives us many more details about the sea-oriented cities. These port cities were influential places. They had many connections to local and international goods. They were places for receiving and distributing money, ideas, and gossip. Tracing Paul's journeys, one will find that when he traveled east to his home base in Antioch or to the temple in Jerusalem, he was on a boat. He took advantage of the prevailing winds to travel quickly by sea instead of by land.

THE KINGDOM OF GOD IN ROME

Luke closes the book of Acts by telling readers that while in Rome, Paul "proclaimed the kingdom of God and taught about the Lord Jesus Christ—with boldness and without hindrance!" (Acts 28:31). Here in the most powerful kingdom of the earth, Paul boldly declared the kingdom of God.

During this time, Paul also wrote several epistles (letters) in the New Testament, including the letter to the church in Philippi. In this letter, he refers to his struggles several times, but he also looks past those struggles and rejoices that even his confinement resulted in good.

> It has become clear throughout the whole palace guard and to everyone else that I am in chains for Christ.
>
> PHILIPPIANS 1:13

The implication is that some of the guards (and people in the palace) responded to some degree to the gospel message. However, Paul's influence clearly extended outside the confines of his locale, as his closing comments in this letter indicate: "All God's people here send you greetings, especially those who belong to *Caesar's household*" (Acts 4:22, emphasis added). Recall what God had told Ananias about Paul after Paul's conversion on the road to Damascus: "This man [Paul] is my chosen instrument to proclaim my name to the Gentiles and their kings and to the people of Israel" (Acts. 9:15). In the final chapter of Acts, we see Paul doing exactly that.

AFTER THE BOOK OF ACTS

There is considerable debate about the final years of Paul's life after the close of Acts. The most accepted theory is that after two years of house arrest, Paul was released and allowed to travel again. During this fourth missionary journey (as some have called it), Paul traveled throughout the Mediterranean:

1. Macedonia (1 Tim. 1:3)
2. Troas (2 Tim. 4:13)

3. Miletus (2 Tim. 4:20)
4. Crete (Titus 1:5)
5. Nicopolis (Titus 3:12)
6. Possibly Spain. (The early church father Clement asserted that Paul did fulfill his desire to go to Spain, expressed in Romans 15:28, but whether the visit actually took place is still uncertain.)

Eventually, Paul went back to Rome, but it may not have been voluntary. It has been suggested that Paul was arrested while in Nicopolis, but the evidence is uncertain. What we do know is that by the time Paul returned to Rome, the widespread persecution of Christians by Emperor Nero had already begun. It's entirely possible that by this time, the apostle Peter had been martyred in Rome.

Ostian Way, Rome, the traditional location of Paul's martyrdom

Paul's imprisonment this time was not house arrest. Rather, it is believed to have been in the cold, infamous Mamertine Prison, where Peter might also have been held. We do have some information about Paul's final days based on Paul's last letter to Timothy. From this very personal, heartfelt letter, we know that Paul was visited by Onesiphorus, who "often refreshed me and was not ashamed of my chains" (2 Tim. 1:16–17). But we also know that Paul had been abandoned by many Christians as he faced trial (2 Tim. 4:10, 16). Luke alone was still with Paul, although Paul expressed the hope that he would see John Mark again when Timothy came to visit (2 Tim. 4:11).

Historical evidence agrees that Paul was executed in Rome, probably by beheading, sometime between AD 66 and 68. But that did not put an end to his ministry. Through his letters in the New Testament and his detailed story in Acts, Paul still ministers to us today.

Throughout the latter thirty years of his life, Paul courageously faced his God-given mission to proclaim the gospel of new and eternal life in Christ Jesus the Savior. That Paul would spread the gospel wasn't the only prophecy given to Ananias about Paul in Acts 9. Look at verse 16: "I [the Lord] will show [Paul] how much he must suffer for my name." Paul knew that hardship for the sake of Jesus awaited him. The Lord had chosen him, and Paul had chosen to go wherever the Lord would lead, even when that path led to suffering. While in prison, facing imminent death, Paul learned to be content and joyful in his circumstances because of the peace he had through Christ. He knew—and could reassure the church in Philippi—that "My God will meet all your needs according to the riches of his glory in Christ Jesus" (Phil. 4:19).

CHAPTER 5

Who's Who in the Book of Acts

Aeneas

ACTS 9:32–35

Aeneas was a citizen of Lydda who was paralyzed and spent eight years bedridden (Acts 9:33). When Peter met him, he said, "Jesus Christ heals you. Get up and roll up your mat." The writer of Acts says as a result of this miracle, "all those who lived in Lydda and Sharon saw him and turned to the Lord" (Acts 9:35).

Agabus

ACTS 11:27–28; 21:10–14

Agabus was among a group of prophets who traveled from Antioch to Jerusalem while Paul and Barnabas were there. He prophesied that a famine would spread through the Roman empire, which the writer of Acts states happened during the reign of Claudius (AD 41–54). Later, he prophesied about Paul's arrest in Jerusalem, tying his own hands and feet with Paul's belt and saying, "In this way the Jewish leaders in Jerusalem will bind the owner of this belt and will hand him over to the Gentiles" (Acts 21:11).

The Prophecy of Agabus by Louis Chéron (1687)

Agrippa I

ACTS 12:1–24

Called "King Herod" in Acts, he was the grandson of Herod the Great and ruled Galilee from AD 39–44. He arrested members of the church in Jerusalem and executed James, the brother of John (Acts 12:2). Due to the Jews' positive reaction to James's death, Herod arrested Peter, who was then miraculously freed from prison by an angel. Herod was later struck dead by an angel when he refused to correct an audience who worshiped him after he gave a public address (Acts 12:21–23).

Agrippa II

ACTS 25:13–27; 26:1–32

Also known as Herod Agrippa, or Agrippa II, he was the son of Agrippa I. He and his sister Bernice listened closely to Paul's testimony during his imprisonment in Caesarea and declared that had Paul not already appealed to Caesar, he could have been freed.

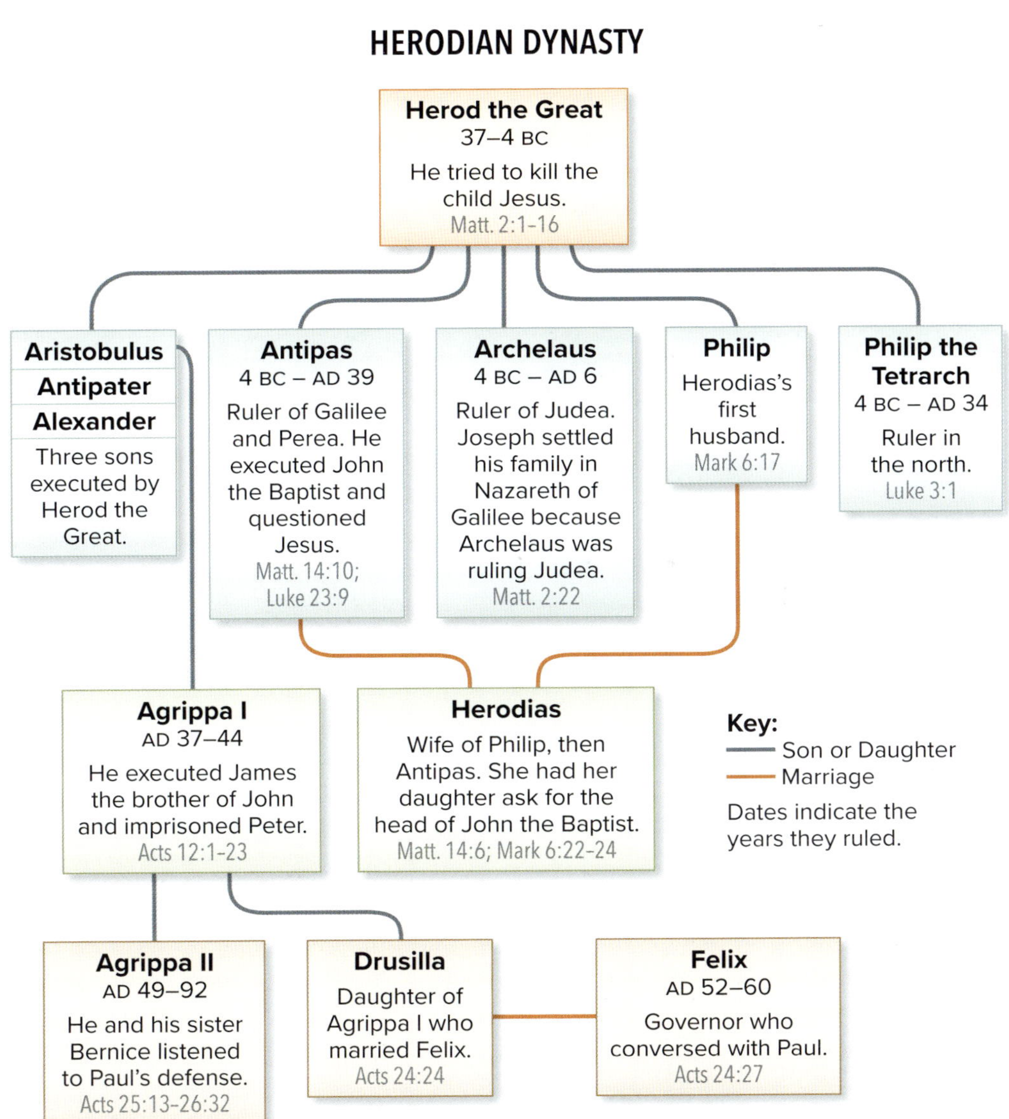

Ananias and Sapphira

ACTS 5:1–11

Early converts to Christianity, this husband and wife sold their possessions and gave part of the money to the apostles. However, they claimed that they gave the apostles all the money they gained. Peter, through the Holy Spirit, knew they were lying; when he accused them of falsehood, they each fell down dead.

Ananias restoring the sight of Saint Paul by Pietro da Cortona (c. 1631)

Ananias of Damascus

ACTS 9:10–19; 22:6–16

A Christian living in the city of Damascus, Ananias received a vision from the Lord telling him to find Saul. After protesting, Ananias went to the house where Saul was staying to lay hands on him, healing his blindness and telling him to be baptized.

Ananias the high priest

ACTS 23:1–5; 24:1–21

He was high priest from AD 47–59 after being appointed by Herod. He was known for his cruelty and ordered Paul to be struck in the face when the apostle testified before the Sanhedrin before his arrest in Jerusalem. Paul accused him of being a hypocrite and a "whitewashed wall" (Acts 23:3). Later, Ananias traveled to Caesarea with some other Jewish leaders to testify against Paul in front of Felix, the Roman governor at the time.

Apollos

ACTS 18:24-26; 19:1

Apollos was a learned Jew from Alexandria in Egypt. Aquila and Priscilla met him in Ephesus, where he was preaching the gospel to the citizens there. Once they filled in the gaps in his knowledge of the gospel, he went on to be a missionary in Achaia.

Aquila and Priscilla

ACTS 18:1–26

These early converts to Christianity were tentmakers, like the apostle Paul. They traveled to Syria with Paul, and when he left Ephesus they stayed behind to minister in the church there, eventually sharing the gospel with Apollos. Paul mentions this couple in letters to Rome, Corinth, and his student Timothy, indicating that they remained important ministry partners.

Aristarchus

ACTS 19:28–29; 20:1–4; 27:2

One of Paul's traveling companions, he was a Macedonian from Thessalonica. He was seized along with Gaius by the mob in Athens who rioted in the name of Artemis. He went with Paul to Macedonia and Troas after the riot in Athens, and later accompanied Paul again on his final journey to Rome.

Bar-Jesus

ACTS 13:6–12

Elymas struck blind by Rafael Sanzio

Also called Elymas, he was a Jewish sorcerer and false prophet who Paul and Silas encountered in Paphos during Paul's first missionary journey. He worked for Sergius Paulus, the Roman proconsul, who summoned Paul and Barnabas in order to hear about the gospel. When Bar-Jesus tried to turn the proconsul against Christianity, Paul called him "a child of the devil and an enemy of everything that is right" (Acts 13:10). Bar-Jesus was cursed with temporary blindness, and when Sergius Paulus saw this happen, he believed the gospel.

Barnabas

ACTS 4:36; 9:26–27; 11–15

Barnabas Portrait at Old monastery of St. Barnabas at Cyprus Famagusta, Northern Cyprus

This Levite from the island of Cyprus was called Barnabas, which means "son of encouragement," by the apostles, though his real name was Joseph. When he is introduced in the book of Acts, he has sold some property in order to give the money to the disciples (Acts 4:36–37). Later, he brought Saul of Tarsus (who became known as Paul) to the apostles for the first time when other members of the church refused to believe Saul's conversion (Acts 9:26–27). He and Paul spent a year serving together in Syrian Antioch, where the word "Christian" was first used to describe followers of Jesus. The duo also led the first missionary journey from Antioch in Acts 13–14.

Bernice

ACTS 25:13–27; 26:1–32

She was the daughter of Herod Agrippa I, and the sister of Herod Agrippa II. She traveled with Agrippa II to Caesarea and heard Paul's testimony along with her brother and Festus, the Roman governor.

Claudius Lysias

ACTS 23:12–35

Claudius Lysias was the Roman commander in Jerusalem when Paul arrived in the city for the last time. He arrested Paul in Jerusalem to prevent him being killed by a mob. When Paul's nephew made him aware of a Jewish plot to kill Paul, Claudius Lysias sent him from Jerusalem to Caesarea with a military escort and wrote a letter to Felix, the Roman governor, asking him to hear the accusations against Paul.

Cornelius

ACTS 10:1–48; 11:1–18

Cornelius was a Roman centurion in the Italian Regiment (Acts 10:1). He is described in Acts 10:2 as "devout and God-fearing" and was known as a generous and prayerful man. While he was living in Caesarea, he received a vision from God instructing him to find the apostle Peter. When his men found Peter in the city of Joppa, the apostle had just received his own vision from God in which he was instructed three times to kill and eat food that was considered unclean according to Jewish law (Acts 10:9–16). Peter preached the gospel to Cornelius, who began speaking in tongues. This confirmed that the Holy Spirit blessed gentiles who heard the gospel as well as Jews. Following this event, Cornelius and his household were baptized by Peter. Later, Peter was criticized by believers in Jerusalem for baptizing gentiles, but when he told the story of his vision and Cornelius's conversion, his audience began praising God for granting eternal life to gentiles (Acts 11:1–18).

Vision of Cornelius the Centurion by Gerbrand van den Eeckhout (1664)

Crispus

ACTS 18:8

Crispus was a leader of the synagogue in Corinth where Paul preached on his second missionary journey. He and his family became Christians after hearing Paul speak.

Damaris

ACTS 17:34

She became a Christian after Paul proclaimed the gospel at the altar dedicated to an unknown God at a meeting of the Areopagus, a Roman governing council, in Athens.

Demetrius

ACTS 19:23–41

Demetrius was a silversmith in Athens who made shrines to Artemis. He assembled a group of Athenian craftsmen who made a similar living and convinced them to riot because Paul was preaching that "gods made by human hands are no gods at all" (Acts 19:26). The mob he incited kidnapped Gaius and Aristarchus, who were traveling with Paul, and held them in the theater in Athens, while Paul's other friends kept him from entering the theater out of concerns for his safety. Eventually, the crowd was calmed by the city clerk, who encouraged them to bring their grievances to the courts rather than rioting.

Dionysius

ACTS 17:34

Dionysius was a member of the Areopagus, a Roman governing council. He became a Christian after Paul proclaimed the gospel at the altar dedicated to an unknown God at a meeting of the Areopagus in Athens.

Dionysius Hosios Loukas monastery

Dorcas

ACTS 9:36–42

Also known as Tabitha, she lived in Joppa and was known for her generosity and kindness to the poor. When she died of an illness, Peter was called from nearby Lydda to come bring her back to life. Because of this miracle, many people in Joppa became Christians.

Erastus

ACTS 19:21–22

He worked with Paul and was sent to Macedonia with Timothy while Paul continued traveling to Jerusalem.

Ethiopian Official

ACTS 8:26–38

This official was in charge of the Ethiopian queen's treasury. While returning home after having traveled to Jerusalem to worship, he encountered Philip, who was on the same travel route after receiving a message from an angel. The official asked Philip to explain the book of Isaiah to him, and Philip shared the gospel, prompting the man to ask to be baptized.

Eunice

ACTS 16:1

The mother of Timothy, she was a Jewish Christian who lived in Lystra. In his second letter to Timothy, Paul talks about her "sincere faith," which she had taught to Timothy since he was an infant (2 Tim. 1:5).

Eutychus

ACTS 20:7–12

Eutychus fell asleep while listening to Paul preach in a third-story room and died after falling from the window at around midnight. When Paul put his arms around him, however, he returned to life. Paul then continued teaching for the rest of the night.

Felix

ACTS 23:23–35; 24:1–27

The Roman governor of Judea from AD 52–58, he kept Paul in prison for two years in hopes of being bribed to let him go. The writer of Acts also mentions that Felix was "well acquainted" with Christianity (Acts 24:22). Felix was married to Drusilla, the daughter of Herod Agrippa I.

Festus

ACTS 24:27; 25:1–27; 26:1–32

Porcius Festus replaced Felix as governor of Judea in AD 58. When he became governor, the chief priests and leaders in Jerusalem brought their case against Paul to him and asked that Paul be transferred to Jerusalem so they could question him, although they were again planning to ambush him before he arrived. Festus instead told the Jewish leaders that they could accompany him to Caesarea to question Paul. When he asked Paul if he would go to Jerusalem as a favor to the Jews, Paul appealed to Caesar. Later, Festus listened to Paul's testimony of faith with King Agrippa II and Bernice, Agrippa's sister, before Paul was brought to Rome.

Gaius

ACTS 19:28–29; 20:1–4

This man was seized along with Aristarchus by the mob in Athens who rioted in the name of Artemis. He is probably the same Gaius who is said to be from Derbe, who travels with Paul to Macedonia after the riot in Athens and then went ahead to Troas.

Gallio

ACTS 18:12–17

The Roman proconsul of Achaia from AD 51–52, he heard accusations against Paul from the Jews in Corinth, who claimed that Paul was "persuading the people to worship God in ways contrary to the law" (Acts 18:13). Gallio dismissed the case before Paul could defend himself, saying that he would only get involved if a "serious crime" had been committed, rather than an offense against Jewish law (Acts 18:14–15). After Gallio sent them away, the Jews accusing Paul beat a leader in the synagogue named Sosthenes. Gallio still refused to interfere.

Gamaliel

ACTS 5:27–40; 22:3

Gamaliel was a respected scholar and Pharisee who convinced the Sanhedrin not to execute the apostles by arguing that if what they preached was false, it would quickly die out on its own, and if it was true, interfering with their message would be "fighting against God" (Acts 5:34–39). While defending himself before a violent crowd in Jerusalem, Paul revealed that he received a Pharisee's education under Gamaliel before his conversion to Christianity (Acts 22:3).

Herod

See *Agrippa I* and *Agrippa II.*

James, the apostle

ACTS 2:1–14, 12:1–2

James was part of Jesus' inner circle and the brother of John. This apostle (not to be confused with James son of Alphaeus) is mentioned in Acts 1:13 as part of the group of Jesus' followers who prayed together after Jesus ascended. He was present with the rest of the apostles on Pentecost (Acts 2:14), and again when they defended their faith before the Sanhedrin and were subsequently flogged in Acts 5. James was martyred under Herod Agrippa I after the king arrested members of the church in order to torture them (Acts 12:1–2).

James, Jesus' brother

ACTS 15:12–21; 21:17–19

The brother of Jesus, James became the leader of the church in Jerusalem. He is most likely the author of the epistle of James in the New Testament. In Acts 15, he supported Paul's case for accepting gentiles as members of the church. He is again mentioned in Acts 21:18 as being present when Paul went to see the church elders in Jerusalem after his third missionary journey.

JAMES THE JUST

In the early fourth century AD, the church historian Eusebius (relying on the memories of Hegesippus, who lived shortly after the apostles) referred to James, one of Jesus' brothers, as "James the Just." He also mentioned him by the nickname "camel knees" because James is said to have prayed so much that he developed calluses on his knees. James is believed to be the author of the epistle that bears his name, one of the earliest New Testament letters (c. AD 49). Church tradition says James was martyred in Jerusalem in AD 62.

James, the brother of Jesus

Here is what the Bible says about him:

- James is first mentioned in the New Testament in Mark 6:3 as one of Jesus' brothers.
- During Jesus' ministry, James was not a follower of his brother (John 7:5).
- James personally saw the resurrected Christ (1 Cor. 15:7).
- After Jesus' ascension into heaven, James was among the believers who gathered for a focused time of prayer (Acts 1:14).
- When the apostle Peter left Jerusalem, James became viewed as the church leader in the city (Acts 12:17).
- The apostle Paul called James a "pillar" of the church (Gal. 2:9).
- We last see James in the book of Acts meeting with Paul and his fellow travelers in Jerusalem, just after Paul's third missionary journey: "The next day Paul and the rest of us went to see James, and all the elders were present" (Acts 21:18).

John

ACTS 1–4; 8:14–25

St. John the Evangelist by Josef Kastner

The brother of James, John was part of Jesus' inner circle of disciples in the gospels and is sometimes referred to as "the beloved disciple." With the other disciples, he prayed in the upper room following Jesus' ascension (Acts 1:13) and witnessed the miracle of Pentecost (Acts 2:14). He was present when Peter healed a lame man outside the temple (Acts 3:1–10). They were arrested and put on trial before the Sanhedrin, where they defended themselves by saying, "Which is right in God's eyes: to listen to you, or to him?" (Acts 4:19). Later, John again accompanied Peter to Samaria, where they laid hands on new believers there to receive the Holy Spirit (Acts 8:14–17). He is believed to have written five books in the New Testament: the gospel of John, the three epistles of John, and the book of Revelation. He was eventually exiled to the island of Patmos. According to tradition, he died of old age in Ephesus around AD 100.

Joseph Barsabbas

ACTS 1:15–26

This Joseph, also known as Justus, is only mentioned once in the book of Acts, when he is nominated alongside Matthias to replace Judas Iscariot among the disciples. Traditionally, he is believed to be one of the seventy-two who were sent out to proclaim the coming of Jesus in Luke 10:1–24.

Julius

ACTS 27:1–44

A Roman centurion and member of the Imperial Regiment, he was in charge of bringing Paul, along with several other prisoners, to Rome. He allowed Paul to visit friends at Sidon, but refused to listen when Paul warned him it was too dangerous to sail from Crete. When they did set sail, they were caught in a storm, during which Paul promised the centurion that no one on the ship would die as it was God's will that Paul be tried in Rome. Their ship was wrecked on the island of Malta after fourteen days, and some of the soldiers wanted to kill Paul and the other prisoners to prevent them escaping. Julius prevented this, however, and everyone on board the ship arrived safely on shore.

Lucius of Cyrene

ACTS 13:1–3

He was among a group of prophets and teachers in Antioch of Syria who laid hands on Paul and Barnabas before they set out on Paul's first missionary journey.

Luke

ACTS 16:10–17; 21:1–18; 27:1–37; 28:1–16

The author of both the gospel of Luke and the book of Acts, he was a physician who traveled with Paul. In Acts 16, he indicates that he accompanied Paul on his second missionary journey, at least until Paul and Silas were imprisoned in Philippi. He traveled with Paul all the way to Jerusalem on his third missionary journey, and was shipwrecked with Paul on his journey to Rome. These have become known as the "we" passages in Acts, where the author includes himself in the narrative; for example, "we traveled to Philippi" (Acts 16:12) and "we would sail for Italy" (Acts 27:1).

St. Luke the Evangelist by Josef Kastner

Lydia

ACTS 16:13–15

Lydia was from the city of Thyatira and showed hospitality to Paul in Philippi after she converted to Christianity and was baptized by him. She was a seller of purple cloth, which was only worn by wealthy people due to its high cost.

Manaen
ACTS 13:1

Manaen was among a group of prophets and teachers who laid hands on Paul and Barnabas before they set out on Paul's first missionary journey. He was raised with Herod Antipas.

Mark (John Mark)
ACTS 12:25; 13:5; 15:37–40

St. Mark the Evangelist by Josef Kastner

Also known by his Hebrew name, John, this follower of Christ sheltered Peter in the home he shared with his mother, Mary, after Peter's escape from prison in Acts 12. He began traveling with Paul and Barnabas on Paul's first missionary journey to Antioch (Acts 12:25), though he separated from them when they arrived in Perga of Pamphylia (Acts 13:13). Later, Barnabas wished to take Mark on a second missionary journey, but Paul objected because of Mark's earlier departure. Mark traveled to Cyprus with Barnabas (Acts 15:39). He is the author of the gospel of Mark, the shortest of the four gospels.

Mary, the mother of John Mark
ACTS 12:12

Peter came to her house after an angel miraculously freed him from prison (Acts 12:6–7). When he arrived, a group of people were there praying.

The Curious Case of John Mark

It may have been his cousin Barnabas's connection to Cyprus that enabled John Mark to start the trip with Barnabas and Paul. We are not told exactly why John Mark left shortly into the trip, but it is clear from later passages that Paul felt that he had abandoned them, which would later lead to Paul and Barnabas parting ways (Acts 15:37–40).

Fortunately, the story doesn't end there for John Mark—or Paul, for that matter. John Mark would later return with Barnabas to Cyprus on another missionary trip (Acts 15:39). Years after Barnabas had given him this second chance (much as Barnabas had done for Paul years earlier),

John Mark would help Paul regularly during his imprisonment in Rome. Paul commended him to the Colossian church, saying:

> My fellow prisoner Aristarchus sends you his greetings, as does Mark, the cousin of Barnabas. (You have received instructions about him; if he comes to you, welcome him.)
>
> COLOSSIANS 4:10

Paul was even more complimentary in his final letter to Timothy:

> Get Mark and bring him with you, because he is helpful to me in my ministry.
>
> 2 TIMOTHY 4:11

John Mark is a wonderful example to us today that failure need not be the end of the story. God can, and will, use us when we're truly ready.

Matthias

ACTS 1:15–26

He was Judas Iscariot's replacement among the disciples. After he and Joseph Barsabbas were nominated to take Judas's place, the disciples prayed for guidance and then cast lots to choose Matthias (Acts 1:23–26). He was the only disciple who was not chosen in person by Jesus, though he is believed to be one of the seventy-two who were sent out to proclaim the coming of Jesus in Luke 10:1–24. According to Greek tradition, Matthias ministered in Cappadocia, which is in modern-day Turkey. Some historians write that he was eventually stoned to death, while others say he was beheaded or crucified.

Saint Matthias

Mnason

ACTS 21:16

A man from Cyprus who was an early disciple of Christianity, he provided lodging for Paul and some other Christians from Caesarea on their way to Jerusalem.

Nicanor

ACTS 6:1–6

Along with six other men, Nicanor was chosen to help distribute food to widows in the early church in Jerusalem.

Nicolas of Antioch

ACTS 6:1–6

He was one of the seven men appointed by the apostles to help care for widows and needy members of the church in Jerusalem. The writer of Acts notes that he was "a convert to Judaism" (Acts 6:6). Some ancient historians claim that he was the founder of a heretical group called the Nicolaitans, who Jesus rebukes the churches of Ephesus and Pergamum for following in Revelation 2:6, 15.

Parmenas

ACTS 6:1–6

Parmenas was one of the seven Spirit-filled men who were appointed to help the apostles minister to members of the church in Jerusalem.

Paul

ACTS 7:58; 8:1–3; 9:1–30; 11–28

Originally known by his Jewish name, Saul of Tarsus, he was a Pharisee who persecuted Christians before converting to Christianity himself. He held the coats of the men who stoned Stephen to death in Acts 7:58 and was on his way to Damascus to imprison Christians in that city when a voice from heaven asked him, "Saul, Saul, why do you persecute me?" (Acts 9:4). Blinded after his miraculous encounter with God, Saul continued to Damascus, where he was healed from his blindness and baptized by Ananias. Immediately, he began to preach the gospel in Damascus and eventually had to be smuggled out of the city. After he proved his sincere faith to the Christians in Jerusalem, he traveled throughout the Roman empire preaching the gospel, going on three missionary journeys with various companions before he was arrested in Jerusalem and eventually brought to Rome. He performed countless miracles, from healing people's illnesses to bringing the dead back to life, and was a strong advocate for the inclusion of gentiles in the early church. Paul is believed to be the author of at least thirteen books in the New Testament, and some believe that he wrote the book of Hebrews in addition to his other epistles. Paul is believed to have been beheaded by Nero sometime after AD 64.

The Conversion of St. Paul on the Road to Damascus by José Ferraz de Almeida Júnior (c. 1890)

Paul's Nephew

ACTS 23:12–22

Nothing is known about this young man except that he was the son of Paul's sister. He discovered a plot between the Sanhedrin, chief priests, and a group of Jews to ambush Paul and kill him. When he told the Roman commander in Jerusalem about this, the commander arranged for Paul to be brought to Caesarea with a military escort for his own safety.

Peter

ACTS 1–5, 8–12, 15:5–11

Peter was the first disciple called by Jesus in the gospels. Originally called Simon, he was named Peter by Jesus. He formed the inner circle of disciples along with James and John. In Acts, he performed several miracles, healing a beggar and raising a woman from the dead. He preached to Cornelius, a gentile, after receiving a vision in which the Lord admonished him, "Do not call anything impure that God has made clean" (Acts 10:15). Later, he urged the other Christian leaders in Jerusalem to accept gentiles into the church without requiring them to be circumcised. When Herod Agrippa imprisoned him in order to execute him, Peter was miraculously freed by an angel of the Lord. Peter is believed to have been martyred in Rome, around AD 66–68, during Emperor Nero's persecution of Christians.

PETER	PAUL
Also called Simon and Cephas which means "the rock" (John 1:42).	Also called Saul, his Hebrew name; Paul is his Roman or Gentile name (Acts 13:9).
A Jew and fisherman from Capernaum in Galilee (Matt. 4:18).	A Jew and Roman citizen by birth from Tarsus in Cilicia (Acts 16:37–38; 21:39).
An "unschooled" man who was trained by Jesus (Acts 4:13).	Trained in the Scriptures by the famous Pharisee Gamaliel (Acts 22:3).
Married (Matt. 8:14).	Unmarried (1 Cor. 7:7–8).
Called by Jesus to be one of the twelve apostles (Matt. 4:18–20; 10:2).	Encountered Jesus on the road to Damascus (Acts 9:1–16). Became an "apostle to the Gentiles" (Gal. 2:8).

PETER	PAUL
Denied knowing Jesus three times when Jesus was arrested (Luke 22:54–62).	Violently persecuted believers before his conversion (Acts 8:3).
Commissioned by the Lord to care for believers; "feed my sheep" (John 21:15–17).	Commissioned by the Lord to proclaim Jesus to gentiles, kings, and Israel (Acts 9:15).
Filled with the Holy Spirit at Pentecost in Jerusalem (Acts 2:4).	Filled with the Holy Spirit in Damascus (Acts 9:17).
Proclaimed Jesus as the Messiah (Matt. 16:16; Acts 2:36).	Proclaimed Jesus as the Messiah (Acts 17:3).
A leader of the church in Jerusalem (Acts 15:6–7).	Launched his missionary journeys from Antioch of Syria (Acts 13:1–3).
Performed miracles, exorcised evil spirits, and raised the dead (Acts 2:3–8; 5:15–16; 9:36–43).	Performed miracles, exorcised evil spirits, and raised the dead (Acts 14:8–10; 19:11–12; 20:9–12).
Received a vision about what "God has made clean" (Acts 10:9–16).	Received a vision of a man from Macedonia (Acts 16:9–10).
Imprisoned for his faith (Acts 12:3–5).	Imprisoned for his faith (Acts 24:27; 2 Tim. 1:16).
Wrote two epistles in the New Testament (1 and 2 Peter) and may have been the main source for the gospel of Mark.	Wrote thirteen epistles in the New Testament.
Martyred in Rome during Emperor Nero's persecution. According to tradition, he was crucified upside down.	Martyred in Rome during Emperor Nero's persecution. According to tradition, he was beheaded.
Jesus had said that even in the manner of his death, Peter would glorify God (John 21:19).	In his last epistle, Paul wrote, "My departure is near. I have fought the good fight, I have finished the race, I have kept the faith" (2 Tim. 4:6–7).

Peter's Spiritual Journey before Acts

When it comes to the twelve apostles, none is described as vividly or featured as prominently in the New Testament as Peter. Because Peter chose to leave his fishing net on the Sea of Galilee and take the risk of following a carpenter's son from Nazareth, he ended up with some amazing stories to tell. (In fact, he is believed to be the primary eyewitness source for Mark's gospel.)

- Though we don't know exactly how many steps he took before his faith faltered and he began to sink, Peter actually walked on water with Jesus (Matt. 14:22–33).
- Peter witnessed Jesus raise a twelve-year-old girl from the dead (Matt. 9:18–26; Mark 5:35–43; Luke 8:49–56).
- He also witnessed the transfiguration, a blinding revelation of Jesus' heavenly glory (Matt. 17:1–9; Mark 9:2–8; Luke 9:28–36).
- When a mob of religious leaders and Roman soldiers came to arrest Jesus, Peter drew his sword and took a wild swing, slicing off a young man's ear. Peter then watched as Jesus miraculously reattached the ear on the spot (Luke 22:50–51; John 18:10).

Peter had confidently confessed Jesus as "the Messiah, the Son of the living God" (Matt. 16:16). Yet in Jesus' darkest hour as he was on trial and condemned to death, Peter's fear got the best of him. He thrice denied even knowing Jesus—a failure of faith that caused him to weep bitterly (Luke 22:54–62). But despite his failure, the Lord did not reject Peter. Upon Christ's resurrection, he restored Peter to his place of servant-leadership among the disciples with the three-fold command to "feed my sheep" (John 21:15–19).

Everything that Peter had witnessed and experienced with the Lord prepared him for the role we see him take in the book of Acts as a bold and fearless leader of the early church.

Sculpture of Peter at the Vatican

Philip the Evangelist

ACTS 6:1–6; 8:4–8, 8:26–40; 21:8–9

Not to be confused with Philip the apostle, this Philip was appointed along with six other men in the early church to help care for widows. He preached and performed miracles in Samaria (Acts 8:4–8). Later, he followed instructions from an angel to go to the road between Jerusalem and Gaza, where he met the Ethiopian official (Acts 8:26–40). He was later referred to as "the evangelist" when Paul stayed with him in Caesarea (21:8). Philip had four daughters who prophesied.

The Baptism of the Eunuch by Rembrandt (1626)

Philippian Jailer

ACTS 16:25–36

He was guarding Paul and Silas in a Philippian prison when they were miraculously freed along with all the other prisoners. Rather than be punished for letting the prisoners escape, he tried to commit suicide but was stopped by Paul, who said, "Don't harm yourself! We are all here!" (Acts 16:28). Upon realizing that the prisoners were all there, the jailer asked Paul and Silas how to be saved. He and his family heard the gospel and were baptized.

Priscilla

See *Aquila and Priscilla.*

Procorus

ACTS 6:1–6

He was one of the seven men appointed by the apostles to help care for widows and needy members of the church in Jerusalem.

Publius

ACTS 28:7–10

He was the chief official on the island of Malta, where Paul and his companions were shipwrecked on their way to Rome. Paul healed Publius's father and many other citizens of Malta who were ill, and in return Publius provided all the supplies Paul needed when he was ready to continue sailing to Rome three months after the shipwreck.

Rhoda

ACTS 12:13–16

When Peter was miraculously freed from prison by an angel in Acts 12 and went to Mary's house, she was the servant girl who found him at the door and was so overjoyed that she forgot to let him in before she ran to tell the other people in the house that he was there.

Sanhedrin

ACTS 4:1–22; 5:17–42; 7:54; 22:30

A *Sanhedrin* (from the Greek *synedrion*) originally meant a local ruling civic body, such as a court or council. By the time Acts was written, probably between AD 70–90, it referred to the highest Jewish judicial council, centered in Jerusalem. The high priest oversaw the Sanhedrin. Its members included elderly aristocratic nobles, chief priests, Sadducees, Pharisees, and scribes. It was undermined and weakened by Herod the Great, but began rising again in power under proconsuls appointed by Rome. The Sanhedrin's decisions reached as far as capital punishment sentencing—though they could not enforce this apart from Roman cooperation. We see this play out in Acts 24, when the Sanhedrin present their case against Paul to the Roman governor Felix.

Sapphira

See *Ananias and Sapphira.*

Saul

See *Paul.*

Secundus

ACTS 20:1–4

A native of Thessalonica, he traveled with Paul from Athens to Macedonia and Troas.

Silas

ACTS 15:22; 18:5

A Jewish Christian who was also a Roman citizen, he accompanied Paul on his second missionary journey. He was arrested with Paul in Philippi. While in prison, they prayed and sang hymns until they were miraculously freed in an earthquake. The jailer who was guarding them believed the gospel and was baptized (Acts 16:25–34). Later in their journey, Paul preached the gospel in Jewish synagogues in Thessalonica and Berea. Silas stayed in Berea with Timothy to serve the new Christians there, while Paul continued on to Athens (Acts 17:14). Eventually, Silas rejoined Paul again in Corinth (Acts 18:5).

Simeon

ACTS 13:1–3

Also called Niger, he was among a group of prophets and teachers who laid hands on Paul and Barnabas before they set out on Paul's first missionary journey.

Simon the Sorcerer

ACTS 8:9–24

He practiced sorcery in Samaria, where people believed he had the power of God. When Philip came to Samaria to preach the gospel and perform miracles, Simon professed to believe in Christ and was baptized. He was later scolded by Peter and John, who came to Samaria to see the work Philip was doing and to lay hands on new believers. Simon offered Peter and John money in exchange for the power to bestow the Holy Spirit on new converts to Christianity. Because he tried to buy the power of God with money, Peter told him, "You have no part or share in this ministry, because your heart is not right before God" (Acts 8:21). Because of Simon's sinful request, the act of trying to buy influence in the church is called "simony."

Simon the Tanner

ACTS 9:43; 10:17

This man's profession was to prepare the skins of animals to be made into leather. Peter stayed at his house, which was by the sea, while in Joppa (Acts 9:43).

Sons of Sceva

ACTS 19:13–20

Sceva was a Jewish high priest whose seven sons were in Ephesus trying to cast out evil spirits by invoking the names of Jesus and Paul. Eventually, a demon spoke back to them, saying, "Jesus I know, and Paul I know about, but who are you?" (Acts 19:15). The man possessed by this demon beat Sceva's sons so badly that many Ephesians who had secretly been Christians confessed their faith publicly, and a group of people who practiced sorcery burned their scrolls.

Sopater

ACTS 20:1–4

The son of Pyrrhus of Berea, he traveled with Paul from Athens to Macedonia and Troas.

Sosthenes

ACTS 18:12–17

This leader of the synagogue in Corinth was beaten by the crowds who brought Paul before Gallio, the Roman proconsul, when Gallio refused to punish Paul for preaching the gospel.

Stephen

ACTS 6:1–6; 8:2

Stephen was part of a group appointed by the apostles to help care for widows in the church. He was singled out by the writer of Acts as a man who was "full of faith and of the Holy Spirit" (Acts 6:5). Accused of blasphemy by Jews who were upset about the miracles he performed, Stephen was stoned to death after delivering a speech to the Sanhedrin explaining how Christ fulfilled Old Testament prophecy. He is the first Christian martyr whose death is recorded in the New Testament.

Tabitha

See *Dorcas.*

Tertullus

ACTS 24:1–6

Tertullus was a lawyer who accompanied the high priest Ananias and other Jewish elders to Caesarea to bring accusations against Paul before Felix, the Roman governor.

Theophilus

ACTS 1:1

Luke addresses Theophilus in the first verse in Acts as the primary recipient of the gospel of Luke and the book of Acts. Though very little is known about Theophilus, he seems to have been a person of high social standing (addressed as "most excellent" in Luke 1:3) and may have been the patron who financed Luke's writing.

Timon

ACTS 6:1–6

He was one of the seven godly men appointed by the apostles to care for widows in the church in Jerusalem.

Timothy

ACTS 16:1–5; 17:14–15; 18:5; 19:21–22; 20:1–4

Saint Timothy

The son of a Jewish woman (named Eunice) and a Greek man, he was circumcised by Paul before accompanying him, along with Silas, on his second missionary journey (Acts 16:1–3). Timothy stayed with Silas in Berea after Paul was forced to leave due to Jews from Thessalonica who came to agitate the crowds they were preaching to (Acts 17:13–15). Timothy later rejoined Paul in Corinth. Timothy is referred to as one of

Paul's "helpers" in Acts 19:22, when he is sent to minister in Macedonia with Erastus while Paul stayed in Asia before traveling to Jerusalem and eventually Rome. Timothy became a pastor in the church of Ephesus and Paul wrote two New Testament epistles encouraging this young pastor (1 and 2 Timothy).

Titius Justus

ACTS 18:7

A "worshiper of God" (Acts 18:7), he lived next door to the synagogue in Corinth. Paul found shelter in his house when the Jews he was preaching to in Corinth became violent. In response to the Jews' opposition, Paul declared, "From now on I will go to the Gentiles" (Acts 18:6).

Trophimus

ACTS 20:1–4; 21:27–29

A native of Ephesus, he traveled with Paul from Athens to Macedonia and Troas. He was with Paul in Jerusalem when Paul was arrested.

Tychicus

ACTS 20:1–4

A traveling companion of Paul's from Asia, he accompanied the apostle from Athens to Macedonia and Troas.

CHAPTER 6

The Holy Spirit

To take the gospel from Jerusalem to the ends of the earth—that is the mission of the church given by the head of the church, Jesus Christ. It's a tall order indeed. But God does not give his people a calling that he will not empower them to carry out. In the book of Acts, Jesus prefaced this mission to his followers by saying, "You will receive power when the Holy Spirit comes on you" (Acts 1:8). This Holy Spirit is a gift promised by God the Father to the followers of Jesus (Acts 1:4). It is this same Spirit who indwells and acts through believers today, continuing the mission of testifying about the good news of life found only through Jesus.

In this chapter, we'll look at who the Holy Spirit is and what he does in the lives of believers, and at the biblical imagery surrounding the Spirit that helps us better understand him.

THE PROMISE OF THE HOLY SPIRIT

Before his death, resurrection, and return to heaven, Jesus promised his disciples that he would send them "another advocate to help you and be with you forever—the Spirit of truth." Then he added, "The world cannot accept him, because it neither sees him nor knows him. But you know him, for he lives with you and will be in you" (John 14:16–17).

Three things are worth noting in Jesus' promise:

1. "Another advocate" means another of the same kind. In other words, as he discussed his own departure, Jesus promised to send his followers a helper who would be like him.

2. Jesus consistently referred to the Spirit as a "he" not an "it." This means that the Spirit is a Person, not a vague power or impersonal force.

3. Jesus assured his disciples that this divine, personal Spirit of truth would never leave them. The Holy Spirit is the Christian's constant companion and advocate. He is God living in those who believe in and follow Jesus.

After Jesus ascended, his disciples were gathered in Jerusalem to pray and celebrate the Jewish festival of Pentecost. The sound of a great rushing wind filled the house they were in. The image of tongues of fire touched each disciple. By the power of the Holy Spirit, the disciples spoke in different languages ("in tongues"). The crowd who had gathered in the city for Pentecost witnessed this power and some were utterly amazed, but others mocked the disciples. Nevertheless, three thousand people believed and were baptized. This incident was the first of many miraculous events that proved the promises of Jesus about the Holy Spirit to be true.

THE PERSON OF THE HOLY SPIRIT

Some people think of the Holy Spirit as impersonal, rather like a force—the energy or power of God. This is probably because Scripture confirms the powerful nature of the Spirit (Luke 4:14) and calls him the power of the Most High and the Spirit of might (Isa. 11:2; Luke 1:35). And yet, unlike an impersonal force, the Holy Spirit has personhood: he can be lied to (Acts 5:3–4); he can be grieved (Eph. 4:30); and he has a name (Matt. 28:19).

Others see the Spirit almost as a feeling—the deep affection that often is experienced among God's people. Maybe this is because Scripture calls him the Spirit of grace, mercy, and comfort (Rom. 8:26; Zech. 12:10; Acts 2:38). However, he is also called the Spirit of truth and justice, indicating that he is more than simply a warm, fuzzy feeling we get when we pray and worship together (John 16:7–8:13).

HOLY SPIRIT OR HOLY GHOST?

The term *Holy Ghost* is used in some older Bible translations, such as the King James Version. But the underlying Greek and Hebrew words translated as *ghost* or *spirit* are the same. The terms *Holy Spirit* and *Holy Ghost* are simply different English translations.

Still others regard the Holy Spirit as the mind, the intellect, behind creation. To be sure, he is the Spirit of wisdom and understanding (1 Cor. 2:11; Isa. 11:2). However, he is more than a cosmic computer that keeps God's plans and purposes on course.

THE TRINITY

To understand who the Holy Spirit is, we need to understand who God is. This means that we need to learn what God reveals in his Word about his triune nature. From the Bible, we can glean the following truths.

TRUTH	MEANING	SCRIPTURE
God is spirit.	His essential nature is immaterial or nonphysical.	"God is spirit, and his worshipers must worship in the Spirit and in truth" (John 4:24).
God is one.	There aren't multiple gods, and God's nature or essence is perfect unity (Isa. 44:6–8; 45:5).	"Hear, O Israel: The LORD our God, the LORD is one" (Deut. 6:4).
God is triune in nature.	The Bible reveals God as a trinity of divine Persons existing in perfect unity. He is one, yet three. This is what people mean when they speak of the Trinity.	"May the grace of the Lord Jesus Christ, and the love of God, and the fellowship of the Holy Spirit be with you all" (2 Cor. 13:14; see also Matt. 3:16-17; 28:19–19; Eph. 4:4–6).

Therefore, the one and only God exists as three distinct persons: God the Father, God the Son, and God the Holy Spirit. Each of the Persons of the Trinity is fully God—and not to be confused with the other Persons of the Trinity.

The Father is God.

- "Yet for us there is but one God, the Father, from whom all things came and for whom we live" (1 Cor. 8:6).
- "One God and Father of all, who is over all and through all and in all" (Eph. 4:6).

The Son is God.

- "In the beginning was the Word [the Son], and the Word was with God, and the Word was God" (John 1:1).

- "But about the Son he says, 'Your throne, O God, will last for ever and ever. A scepter of justice will be the scepter of your kingdom'" (Heb. 1:8).
- See also John 10:30–33; 20:28; Phil. 2:9–11.

The Holy Spirit is God.

- "Now the Lord is the Spirit, and where the Spirit of the Lord is, there is freedom" (2 Cor. 3:17).
- "Then Peter said, 'Ananias, how is it that Satan has so filled your heart that you have lied to the Holy Spirit and have kept for yourself some of the money you received for the land. … You have not lied just to human beings but to God'" (Acts 5:3–4).

With that quick overview, we can answer the question, *Who is the Holy Spirit?*

The Holy Spirit is God. The Holy Spirit is the third Person of the Trinity. "Therefore, go and make disciples of all nations, baptizing them in the name of the Father and of the Son and of the Holy Spirit" (Matt. 28:19).

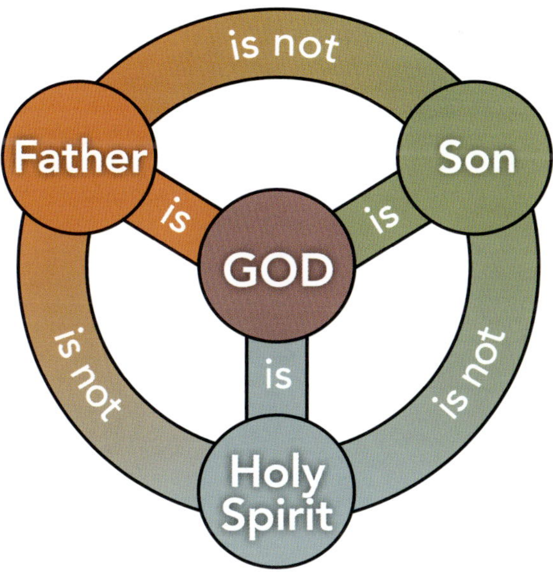

This diagram, often called "the Shield of the Trinity", illustrates how each of the three Persons of the Trinity is God, but each is not identical to the others.

ACTIVITIES OF THE HOLY SPIRIT

In the past, the Holy Spirit:

- Created the world (Gen. 1:2; Ps. 104:30).
- Inspired and superintended the human authors of Scripture (2 Peter 1:21).
- Conceived Jesus (Luke 1:35).
- Resurrected Christ (Rom. 8:11; 1 Peter 3:18).

In the present, the Holy Spirit works in the church in the following ways:

Indwells

When we put our trust in Christ, the Holy Spirit of the living God takes up residence in our lives!

> If the Spirit of him who raised Jesus from the dead is living in you, he who raised Christ from the dead will also give life to your mortal bodies because of his Spirit who lives in you.
>
> ROMANS 8:11

> Do you not know that your bodies are temples of the Holy Spirit, who is in you, whom you have received from God?
>
> 1 CORINTHIANS 6:19

Regenerates

Apart from this spiritual rebirth, we cannot come alive to God (Eph. 2:1–5).

> Flesh gives birth to flesh, but the Spirit gives birth to spirit.
>
> JOHN 3:6

Convicts

The Holy Spirit convinces people of their need to repent from sin and to look to Christ for righteousness.

> When [the Holy Spirit] comes, he will convict the world of its sin, and of God's righteousness, and of the coming judgment.
>
> JOHN 16:8 NLT

Seals

Like a seal of authenticity, the Holy Spirit marks us as God's property.

> And you also were included in Christ when you heard the message of truth, the gospel of your salvation. When you believed, you were marked in him with a seal, the promised Holy Spirit.
>
> EPHESIANS 1:13

Guides

When life is dark and the way is vague, the Holy Spirit is our leader.

> But when he, the Spirit of truth, comes, he will guide you into all the truth. He will not speak on his own; he will speak only what he hears, and he will tell you what is yet to come.
>
> JOHN 16:13

Advocates

The Holy Spirit is the 24/7 counselor and defender of Jesus' followers.

> I will ask the Father, and he will give you another advocate to help you and be with you forever.
>
> JOHN 14:16

Teaches

The Holy Spirit shows us what is right, what is wrong, and how to live.

> But the Advocate, the Holy Spirit, whom the Father will send in my name, will teach you all things and will remind you of everything I have said to you.
>
> JOHN 14:26

Intercedes

Knowing the will of God and the desires of our hearts, the Holy Spirit speaks to God on our behalf.

> In the same way, the Spirit helps us in our weakness. We do not know what we ought to pray for, but the Spirit himself intercedes for us through wordless groans.
>
> ROMANS 8:26

Gives Assurance

In big and small ways, the Holy Spirit confirms that we belong to God and that he is working in us.

> The Spirit himself testifies with our spirit that we are God's children.
>
> ROMANS 8:16

Empowers

We are not called to live for God in our own limited strength. The Holy Spirit is our infinite power source.

> But you will receive power when the Holy Spirit comes on you; and you will be my witnesses in Jerusalem, and in all Judea and Samaria, and to the ends of the earth.
>
> ACTS 1:8

Activities of the Holy Spirit from the Book of Acts

ACTIVITY	BOOK OF ACTS
Aided the ministry of Jesus.	"All that Jesus began to do and to teach until the day he was taken up to heaven, after giving instructions through the Holy Spirit to the apostles he had chosen" (Acts 1:1–2; also 10:38).
Spoke through the biblical writers.	"The Scripture had to be fulfilled in which the Holy Spirit spoke long ago through David" (Acts 1:16; also 4:25; 28:25).
Enabled the speaking in tongues.	"All of them were filled with the Holy Spirit and began to speak in other tongues as the Spirit enabled them" (Acts 2:4; also 19:6).
Filled and empowered believers to speak the word of God.	"They were all filled with the Holy Spirit and spoke the word of God boldly" (Acts 4:31; also 4:8).
Gave wisdom.	"But they could not stand up against the wisdom the Spirit gave him as he [Stephen] spoke" (Acts 6:10).
Revealed the glory of God and Jesus.	"Stephen, full of the Holy Spirit, looked up to heaven and saw the glory of God, and Jesus standing at the right hand of God" (Acts 7:55).
Was received by believers in Jesus.	"Peter and John placed their hands on them, and they received the Holy Spirit" (Acts 8:17).
Directed evangelism.	"The Spirit told Philip, 'Go to that chariot and stay near it'" (Acts 8:29; also 16:6–10).
Encouraged the church.	"Living in the fear of the Lord and encouraged by the Holy Spirit, it [the church] increased in numbers" (Acts 9:31).

ACTIVITY	BOOK OF ACTS
Spoke to believers.	"While Peter was still thinking about the vision, the Spirit said to him, 'Simon, three men are looking for you'" (Acts 10:19; also 13:2).
Was experienced as a baptism.	"John baptized with water, but you will be baptized with the Holy Spirit" (Acts 11:16; also 1:5).
Gave prophecy.	"Agabus stood up and through the Spirit predicted that a severe famine would spread over the entire Roman world" (Acts 11:28; also 19:6).
Guided church decisions.	"It seemed good to the Holy Spirit and to us not to burden you with anything beyond the following requirements" (Acts 15:28).
Compelled believers to act.	"And now, compelled by the Spirit, I [Paul] am going to Jerusalem, not knowing what will happen to me there" (Acts 20:22).
Warned believers.	"I [Paul] only know that in every city the Holy Spirit warns me that prison and hardships are facing me" (Acts 20:23).
Appointed church leaders.	"Keep watch over yourselves and all the flock of which the Holy Spirit has made you overseers" (Acts 20:28).

THE HOLY SPIRIT AND PRAYER

The Spirit of God is the Spirit of prayer. We can only approach God through Christ with the help of the Spirit. Jesus is humanity's only access to God. Since his ascension, Christ has not been physically present on earth; the only way to lay our requests and worship before him, and so before God, is by means of the Holy Spirit.

One of the crucial tasks of the Spirit is to inspire and guide our prayers. When our weaknesses prevent us from relating to God correctly, the Spirit intercedes for us—that is, he pleads our case before God—so we can rest assured that the Spirit is praying alongside us, making our prayers what they ought to be.

> In the same way, the Spirit helps us in our weakness. We do not know what we ought to pray for, but the Spirit himself intercedes for us through wordless groans. And he who searches our hearts knows the mind of the Spirit, because the Spirit intercedes for God's people in accordance with the will of God.
>
> ROMANS 8:26–27

If we understand prayer as communication with God, then we will be able to see it more fully as a dialogue, rather than a monologue on our part. Prayer is a two-way conversation; the other half of our worship before God is God's guidance and clarity of his will to us. Just as we may only reach God in the Spirit through the truth of Christ, so also God's guidance and teaching comes to us only through Christ by means of the Spirit (John 4:24; 14:26; 15:26; 16:12–14).

SYMBOLS OF THE HOLY SPIRIT

By definition, anything that is spiritual is nonphysical, immaterial, invisible. This obviously includes the Holy Spirit. We can't see the Spirit of God with our physical eyes, but we can see the effects of the Spirit. It is for this reason that the Bible uses various symbols—often common, earthly objects—to describe who the Spirit is and what he does.

Wind

In John 3:8, Jesus uses a play on words to inform Nicodemus, a Jewish religious leader, that the Spirit of God is like wind. The Greek word, *pneuma*, which is translated as "Spirit," can also be translated as "wind" or "breath." The Lord's point is that while we can't physically see wind, we can feel a cool breeze or watch a flag whip wildly. As the wind is unpredictable—suddenly kicking up or swirling or changing direction—so the Spirit acts in ways we can't predict. Some days are still—we can't sense even the hint of a "spiritual breeze." Other days, the Spirit moves with sudden, astonishing power, almost like wind shear. Still other times, like a favorable tailwind to a sailor, the Spirit brings us to wonderful destinations.

When the Holy Spirit descended upon believers in Jerusalem, he made his presence known with a sound like a powerful windstorm: "When the day of Pentecost came, they were all together in one place. Suddenly a sound like the blowing of a violent wind came from heaven and filled the whole house where they were sitting" (Acts 2:1–2).

> But when he, the Spirit of truth, comes, he will guide you into all the truth. He will not speak on his own; he will speak only what he hears, and he will tell you what is yet to come. He will glorify me because it is from me that he will receive what he will make known to you.
>
> John 16:13–14

Water

One of the more prominent biblical symbols for the Holy Spirit is water. In biblical times, at the end of the Feast of Tabernacles in Jerusalem, Israel's high priest would pour out (near the altar) a pitcher of water drawn from the Pool of Siloam. This was such a happy occasion—with singing an celebrating and hopeful anticipation of the Messiah's future reign—that Israel's rabbis declared that people who had never witnessed this ritual did not know the true meaning of joy!

During his earthly ministry, Jesus seized upon this ancient tradition to declare his unique ability to quench the deepest thirsts of the human heart (John 7:37–38). He promised to give the Holy Spirit to those who trusted him. And he said that the indwelling Spirit would be like "rivers of living water" flowing from within believers. Perhaps picking up on this idea, the apostle Paul described joy, peace, and hope as qualities that would overflow from the life of a Spirit-led Christian (Rom. 15:13; Gal. 5:22–23). In Acts, the descending of the Spirit upon believers is described as a baptism (Acts 1:5).

Fountains, streams, wells—all these watery images are used to demonstrate the work of the Spirit. Water cleanses and refreshes. It gives life, and, when harnessed correctly, provides great power.

Clothing

After his crucifixion and resurrection, Jesus appeared multiple times to his most devoted followers. On one of those occasions, he told his disciples to take the good news of forgiveness "to all nations." But first, he said, "stay in the city until you have been clothed with power from on high" (Luke 24:49). "Power from on high" is a clear reference to the Holy Spirit (John 16:7–15; Acts 1:8). According to Jesus, the Spirit is something like clothing. Without clothing, we are naked and vulnerable. When we try to live without the power of the Spirit, we are spiritually naked and vulnerable.

Oil

In the Old Testament, newly chosen prophets, priests, and kings were routinely anointed with oil (Ex. 40:11–15; Lev. 8:30; 1 Sam. 10:1–10; 16:13). This ceremony conveyed an important truth to everyone watching: the person upon whom the oil was poured was being set apart for God's holy use. Anointed officials were to live as servants of the one true God. They were to rely on the Spirit of God, not their own power (Zech. 4:1–14).

The New Testament uses this same anointing imagery to speak of Christians (compare Acts 10:38 with Acts 1:8; 2 Cor. 1:21; 1 John 2:20). It is the Holy Spirit who anoints us, setting us apart for God's service:

> While they were worshiping the Lord and fasting, the Holy Spirit said, "Set apart for me Barnabas and Saul for the work to which I have called them."
>
> ACTS 13:2

Seal

In 2 Corinthians 1:22, Paul uses a rich, descriptive phrase to help us understand the Person and work of the Spirit. He calls the third Person of the Trinity God's "seal" on believers (see also Eph. 1:13; 4:30).

What does it mean that God seals Christians with his Spirit? In ancient times, seals were used to show ownership of an item. Seals also served as a means of security and protection. Remember how Pilate told his guards to secure the grave of Jesus by "putting a seal on the stone" (Matt. 27:64–66)? When we speak of the Spirit as a seal, we mean that God owns Christians, and that believers are eternally safe and secure.

Deposit

In saying that God "put his Spirit in our hearts as a deposit" (2 Cor. 1:22), the apostle Paul used a commercial term. The Greek word *arrabon* means "down payment, pledge, or first installment." The presence of the Spirit in our lives is a guarantee that God will finish the work he has started in us. "Being confident of this, that he who began a good work in you will carry it on to completion until the day of Christ Jesus" (Phil. 1:6).

Dove

After Jesus was baptized, witnesses watched the Spirit of God descend on him from heaven "like a dove" (Matt. 3:16; Mark 1:10; Luke 3:22; John 1:32). This doesn't necessarily mean that the Spirit became an actual dove, only that he resembled one. What is the symbolism here? How is God's Spirit like a dove?

Doves are the universal symbol of peace. It is only fitting that Jesus, the "Prince of Peace" (Isa. 9:6) who came to help sinners experience "peace with God" (Rom. 5:1) would be crowned, as it were, with peace at the beginning of his public ministry.

As Jesus said in Matthew 10:16, doves are also a symbol of innocence. How appropriate that the Spirit who is holy would be likened to a creature considered innocent and pure.

Fire

In Old Testament times, the presence of God was often symbolized by fire. God spoke to Moses out of a burning bush (Ex. 3:2). The Israelites knew that God was among them because of the blazing fire over the tabernacle, their worship center (Ex. 40:38). They were guided through the wilderness at night by "a pillar of fire" (Num. 14:14). Sacrifices acceptable to God were sometimes consumed by fire from heaven (Lev. 9:24; 1 Kings 18:38).

In the New Testament, when the Holy Spirit was poured out on those who had put their faith in Jesus, witnesses saw "tongues of fire" coming "to rest on each of them" (Acts 2:3). This demonstrated that God now resided in the hearts of believers! Fire can also be a symbol of judgment, and the Spirit came to convict the world of sin and righteousness and judgment (John 16:8–11). Fire—like in an offering or sacrifice—purifies, and the Holy Spirit came to make us holy: "I bring you the Good News so that I might present you as an acceptable offering to God, made holy by the Holy Spirit" (Rom. 15:16 NLT; see also 1 Peter 1:2).

BAPTISM OF THE HOLY SPIRIT

Before his ascension into heaven, Christ told his followers that "in a few days you will be baptized with the Holy Spirit" (Acts 1:5). Christian groups define the baptism of the Holy Spirit in different ways.

For some Christians, the idea is intimately connected to water baptism and **initiation** into God's family. Jesus' own baptism seems to set the pattern, where water and the Spirit are both evident (Matt. 3:11–17). Paul connects the idea of baptism with being initiated into the church (1 Cor. 12:13).

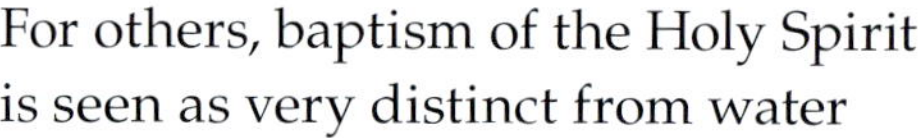

For others, baptism of the Holy Spirit is seen as very distinct from water baptism. Here the emphasis is on an **infusion** of power for ministry. The book of Acts recounts many instances in which this infusion took place apart from water baptism (Acts 2:4; 4:8).

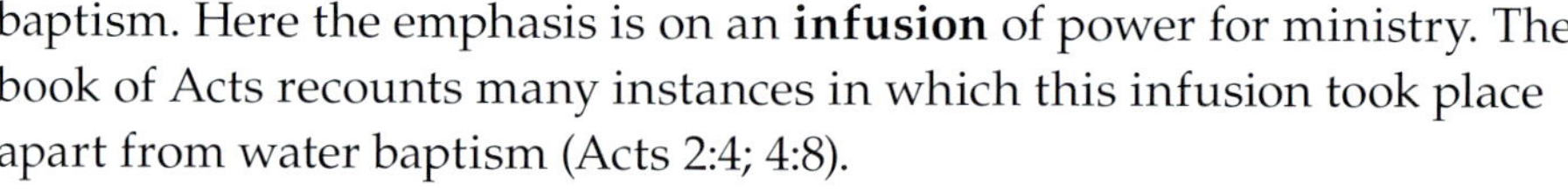

Still others regard the Spirit's work as centering on **identification** with Christ. Paul understands baptism and the work of the Spirit as connecting and conforming us to Christ's life by being baptized into or identified with his death (Rom. 6:3–4).

In fact, all of these—initiation, infusion, and identification—are involved in the work of the Holy Spirit, though they may not all be in view together at one time.

- We are initiated into the life and body of Christ by the regenerating act of the Spirit.
- We are infused with God's power for ministry when the Spirit fills us with himself.
- We are identified with Christ in his life, death, and resurrection as the Holy Spirit transforms us into Christ's image.

All these things may be said to be part of the baptism of the Holy Spirit because different passages in the Bible direct us to each of these. Yet there is a sense in which these diverse works are one work of the same Spirit, though we may experience each at different times in our lives. If we step back from the current Christian disagreements about what the baptism of the Holy Spirit means to get the larger picture of this singular, timeless work of the Spirit, we may come to see it as involving the entire work of the Spirit in, through, and on behalf of humanity.

THE TEMPLE OF THE HOLY SPIRIT

In Old Testament times, the temple (and the tabernacle before it) was the place where God's special presence resided. It was the holy sanctuary where God's people met with their holy God.

In the New Testament, all believers together—the church—are called God's temple. As the apostle Paul says, "Don't you know that you yourselves are God's temple and that God's Spirit dwells in your midst?" (1 Cor. 3:16). Not only are believers together the temple, but our individual bodies are also called temples: "Do you not know that your bodies are temples of the Holy Spirit, who is in you, whom you have received from God?" (1 Cor. 6:19).

The Spirit of God that dwelled in the temple in ancient times now indwells believers in Jesus. Knowing this truth should encourage us to "honor God with [our] bodies" (1 Cor. 6:20). Our bodies—both individually and together as the body of Christ, the church—should not be used for sinfulness and immorality, but to honor God by being receptive to the work of the Spirit whose presence makes us holy. When Paul (Saul) was filled with the Holy Spirit, it transformed his whole being—from a zealous persecutor of the church to its most famous Christian missionary: "Placing his hands on Saul, he said, 'Brother Saul, the Lord—Jesus, who appeared to you on the road as you were coming here—has sent me so that you may see again and be filled with the Holy Spirit'" (Acts 9:17).

GIFTS OF THE SPIRIT

All the activities of the Holy Spirit—from interceding and advocating to guiding and empowering—point to his main role: to glorify Christ (John 16:14). Similarly, the goal of our own ministries should be to glorify Christ. How do we do this? By serving the body of Christ and helping it grow up (mature) and grow out (expand). But how do we do this most effectively? Through the work of the Holy Spirit, especially his work of enabling and equipping each one of us with special abilities for serving.

Ministries are activities believers do that serve the church and allow it to grow. Through the Spirit, God gives gifts—in the sense of presents—to each believer. These gifts are called spiritual gifts because they are given by the Spirit: "[The Spirit] distributes them to each one, just as he determines" (1 Cor. 12:11). With these tools, we serve God and minister to others.

When Paul explained what the church is and how it works, he used the image of a body. His teaching in 1 Corinthians 12 and Romans 12 speaks about the organic unity of Christ's body, the church. The Holy Spirit gives gifts with specific spiritual functions for the benefit of the entire church. The gifts complement each other and work together for the common good, much as the parts of the body are designed to do.

> For just as each of us has one body with many members, and these members do not all have the same function, so in Christ we, though many, form one body, and each member belongs to all the others. We have different gifts, according to the grace given to each of us.
>
> ROMANS 12:4–6

The Spirit is God's gift to us as individuals and as a body (Acts 2:38; 10:45). Individuals who have come into this life, the life of Christ, are automatically part of a larger whole. These gifts operate as parts of a whole. Gifting, reception of the Spirit, and membership in the body of Christ are all connected in the life of the believer and for the good of the whole church.

What Are Gifts?

The English word gift has two meanings:

1. Something that is given freely and without charge, such as a present for a birthday.

2. A special ability or talent, such as playing piano or learning languages.

Both meanings help us understand spiritual gifts:

1. Spiritual gifts are unearned and undeserved. They are God's generous gifts to us.

2. Spiritual gifts involve special talents and abilities, particularly for ministries like healings, miracles, or speaking in tongues.

However, the emphasis of the New Testament is not on the abilities themselves but on how they function in the ministries (services) of the church. As we think about spiritual gifts, keep in mind that what makes them spiritual is that they come from the Holy Spirit, and what makes them gifts is that the Holy Spirit freely gives them to us. Spiritual gifts are not meant to be stored or publicized. They are meant to be used for the service of others.

Four Lists of Spiritual Gifts

GIFT	ROM. 12:6-8	1 COR. 12:8-10	1 COR. 12:28-30	EPH. 4:11
Pastoring				✔
Teaching	✔		✔	✔
Encouraging (Exhortation)	✔		✔	
Prophecy	✔	✔	✔	✔
Healings		✔	✔	
Leadership	✔			
Guidance			✔	
Message of Wisdom		✔		
Message of Knowledge		✔		
Miracles		✔	✔	
Service/Helps	✔		✔	
Acts of Mercy	✔			
Giving	✔			
Speaking in and/or Interpreting Tongues		✔	✔	
Faith		✔		
Evangelism				✔
Distinguishing between Spirits		✔		
Apostleship			✔	✔

Pastoring, Teaching, and Encouraging

ROM. 12:7–8; 1 COR. 12:28–29; EPH. 4:11

Traditionally, the ministry of pastors is closely connected to that of teaching. In addition to caring for the members of each church, the other crucial role of pastors is to explain the apostolic teachings to believers. However, many people can thrive as teachers without having to become pastors. Teaching is a vital ministry of the body of Christ. Beyond giving information, teaching allows people to deepen their relationship with God and equips believers to be aware of false teachings that they might encounter.

Closely connected to other gifts, encouraging (or exhortation) means that a person comes alongside another with words of comfort, consolation, and counsel to help them be all God wants them to be.

Examples in Acts

Priscilla and Aquila taught Apollos, a new believer, the way of God more accurately (Acts 18:26). In Paul's farewell address to the elders of Ephesus, he reminds them that it is the Holy Spirit who made them overseers to shepherd the Lord's flock (Acts 20:28).

Prophecy

ROM. 12:6; 1 COR. 12:10, 28; EPH. 4:11

Prophets played an important role in the formation of the early church. Their activities included:

- Announcing what will happen (Acts 11:28).
- Encouraging believers (Acts 15:32).
- Making known the mysteries of salvation (Eph. 3:5–6).

Some Christians believe that the "office" of prophet ended with the close of the era of the apostles. In 1 Thessalonians 5:20–22, believers are told not to despise prophecy, but to "test everything" to see if it is truly from God.

The apostle Paul reminds believers that even a gift like prophecy is useless without love (1 Cor. 13:2).

Examples in Acts

There were prophets in the church at Antioch (Acts 13:1). Judas and Silas were prophets (Acts 15:32), as were Philip's four daughters (Acts 21:8–9). A prophet named Agabus prophesied to Paul (Acts 21:10–11).

Healings

1 COR. 12:9, 28, 30

Healings, like other miracles, were a demonstration of God's power that validated apostolic authority. The specific "office" of healer (if there was ever one) may have ended with the apostolic age. However, Christians continue to believe that God can and does heal as a response to prayer.

Examples in Acts

Peter and John healed a beggar who was lame from birth (Acts 3:1–8). Even Peter's shadow falling on people brought healing (Acts 5:12–16). Philip performed miracles and cast out demons (Acts 8:6–7). Peter raised Tabitha from the dead (Acts 9:36–42). Paul healed a lame man, Publius's father, and others (Acts 14:8–10; 28:7–9).

Leadership and Guidance

ROM. 12:8, 1 COR. 12:28

Although traditionally these gifts have been related to the ministry of elders in the church, the context of the passages suggests that they are also meant for all believers. These ministries are applicable to many areas of church life:

- Goals for the church
- Teaching

- Evangelism
- Acts of mercy and service

Examples in Acts

When the first Christians had a crucial decision to make about how to include gentiles into what had been largely a Jewish congregation, the church leaders in Jerusalem relied on the Holy Spirit to help them decide how to guide the church through this complicated issue (Acts 15).

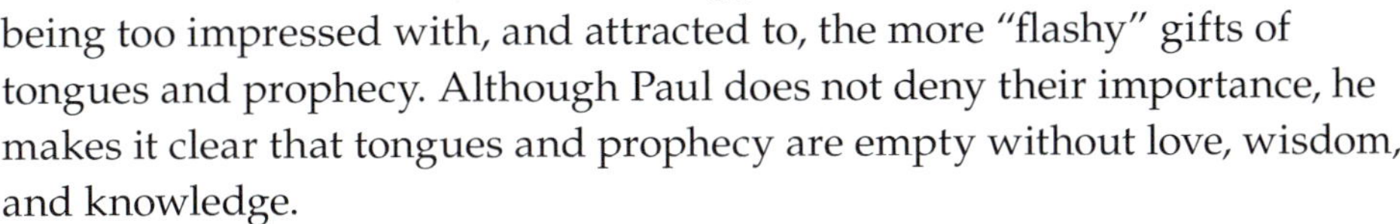

Message of Wisdom and Message of Knowledge

1 COR. 12:8

We must understand these two gifts in the context of the whole letter to the Corinthians. The Corinthian church seems to have struggled with being too impressed with, and attracted to, the more "flashy" gifts of tongues and prophecy. Although Paul does not deny their importance, he makes it clear that tongues and prophecy are empty without love, wisdom, and knowledge.

Wisdom is the discerning and understanding of God's doings in the world and the way the world functions. This is a critical ministry that allows all ministries and gifts of the church to work in harmony and unity. Knowledge allows believers to understand and explain God's revelation to others.

Examples in Acts

The seven men chosen to administer the food distribution in Jerusalem are described as being "full of the Spirit and wisdom" (Acts 6:3). Apollos had a thorough "knowledge of the Scriptures" (Acts 18:24).

Miracles

1 COR. 12:10, 28–29

For the apostle Paul, miracles existed to validate the message of the apostles: "I persevered in demonstrating among you the marks of a true apostle, including signs, wonders and miracles" (2 Cor. 12:12). Some Christians believe that the need for these miracles for validation ended with the passing of the apostles. However, all Christians affirm the possibility and existence of miracles from God today.

Examples in Acts

Philip performed many signs and wonders that validated his message of the gospel (Acts 8:6–7). Paul miraculously blinded the sorcerer Elymas (Acts 13:6–11). Paul and Barnabas performed signs and wonders on their missionary journeys (Acts 14:3).

Service/Helps, Acts of Mercy, and Giving

1 COR. 12:28; ROM. 12:7–8

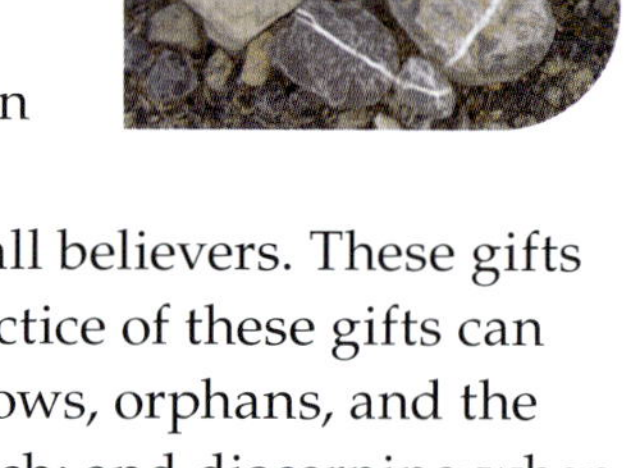

These different gifts are so closely related that some tend to assign them to the tasks of deacons in the church. However, the overall context of these passages suggests that they are also activities for all believers. These gifts are crucial for the maturity of the church. The practice of these gifts can vary, and include things like: offering help to widows, orphans, and the poor; giving aid for the daily activities in the church; and discerning when individuals or groups are in need of help to carry on their ministries.

Examples in Acts

Christians in Antioch took up a special collection to help believers in Judea facing a severe famine (Acts 11:27–30). After the Lord opened Lydia's heart to the gospel, she opened her home to Paul and the other traveling missionaries (Acts 16:13–15). Timothy and Erastus are identified as Paul's "helpers" during his missionary journeys (Acts 19:22).

Speaking in Tongues and Interpreting Tongues

1 COR. 12:10, 28, 30

The apostle Paul did not discourage speaking in tongues—in fact, he urged the Corinthian church leaders to allow it (1 Cor. 14:39). However, Paul did correct an error in the church:

- Some in the Corinthian church were too enchanted with the gift of speaking in tongues.
- Paul reminded them that speaking in tongues without love is like a "resounding gong or a clanging cymbal" (1 Cor. 13:1).
- Paul's main concern is the edification of the church as a whole, as a body.

Today, Christians differ on whether the ministry of speaking in tongues has stopped or continues. Either way, Paul makes it clear that the unity of the body of Christ is far more important than speaking, or not speaking, in tongues.

Examples in Acts

The most famous example is at Pentecost when the Holy Spirit descended upon believers and the church was born: "All of them were filled with the Holy Spirit and began to speak in other tongues as the Spirit enabled them" (Acts 2:4).

Faith

1 COR. 12:9

This spiritual gift of faith is not "saving faith," which every believer has (Eph. 2:8), or the daily faith necessary for the Christian life. Instead, it is faith that complements the other gifts and allows them to be daring and active. When the ministries of the church face odds that overwhelm most people, this faith challenges, encourages, and reminds people that we serve a powerful God who owns and controls all things.

Examples in Acts

Stephen is described as "a man full of faith" (Acts 6:5). Paul encouraged his dejected shipmates stranded at sea to keep their courage, for he had faith that God would get them all to Rome and not one would die, just as God had promised (Acts 27:22–25).

Evangelism

EPH. 4:11

Evangelism is sharing the good news of the gospel. It is the privilege and responsibility of every believer. Some people have a special, God-given ability to present the message of salvation in a clear, simple, and engaging way. Those who fit in this ministry can provide leadership to all believers to carry out the task of evangelism.

Examples in Acts

Peter took the lead among the apostles and preached the gospel to thousands of Jews gathered in Jerusalem for the festival of Pentecost (Acts 2:14–41). Philip the evangelist explained the good news of Jesus to the Ethiopian official who was reading from book of Isaiah (Acts 8:34–35; 21:8).

Distinguishing between Spirits

1 COR. 12:10

In the context of the letter to the Corinthians, distinguishing (or discerning) between spirits may refer to two activities.

The first activity is the ability to discern when a prophecy truly comes from God. (Christians who believe that the gift of prophecy has ceased view this part of discerning as no longer necessary; see 1 Cor. 13:8.)

The second activity is the ability to discern when a teaching fits in with God's will and comes from the leading of the Holy Spirit. It also includes the ability to know when a new teaching contradicts the basic teachings of the Christian faith.

Examples in Acts

The Berean Jews examined the Scriptures daily to see if Paul's message was true (Acts 17:11). A man named Simon amazed the people of Samaria with his sorcery for many years, but he could not fool Peter and John when they arrived in Samaria and saw through his tricks and into his heart (Acts 8:9–24).

Apostleship

1 COR. 12:28–29; EPH. 4:11

There is more than one kind of apostle in the New Testament:

- The first kind refers to those Jesus called and set apart, who witnessed his life and ministry. These are the twelve disciples, and also include apostles like Paul (1 Cor. 9:1; 15:5–9; Gal. 2:8).
- The second kind of apostle includes those who were especially appointed as missionaries to spread the gospel (1 Thess. 2:6).

Examples in Acts

Believers in Jerusalem appointed Matthias as an apostle to replace Judas Iscariot (Acts 1:23–26). Barnabas was set apart by the Holy Spirit for missionary work and was identified as an apostle (Acts 13:2–3; 14:14).

PHOTOS AND ILLUSTRATIONS

Images used under license from Shutterstock.com: John Ilich, cover; In Green, cover; S.Borisov, cover; LittlePerfectStock, cover; Perfect Lazybones, p. 5, 65; haveseen p. 6; The Stoning of St. Stephen, Church Kostel Svateho Cyrila Metodeje by S. G. Rudh (1896), Renata Sedmakova, p. 9; Nils Prause, p. 13; Vladimir Sazonov, p. 14; Wirestock Creators, p. 15; Triff, p. 27, 95; Grzegorz Zdziarski, p. 28; otnaydur, p. 30, cover; Pit Stock, p. 31; Valery Rokhin, p. 32; Book of Acts King James Version, Chiang Mai, Thailand (March 30, 2021) by aradapollawat, p. 34; film.plus, p. 38; mhellal, p. 43, 123; Phant, p. 45; Mikhail Semenov, p. 53; View of Ein Kerem near Jerusalem by TaliV, p. 54; etienneb07, p. 60; Robert Hoetink, p. 63; Sopotnicki, p. 73; Izabela Miszczak, p. 76; St. Paul at the Council of Jerusalem, All Saints' Anglican Church (19th century), Renata Sedmakova, p. 78; Milan Gonda, p. 80; okanakdeniz, p. 83; Fresco of Life of Paul: Paul Is Arrested, Basilica of Saint Paul, Rome, Zvonimir Atletic, p. 87; Richard A McMillin, p. 91; Fabio Lamanna, p. 93; John, Luke, and Mark by Josef Kastner in Carmelites Church, Vienna, Renata Sedmakova, pp. 107-109; St. Barnabas at Cyprus Famagusta, Cyprus, hmxphotography, p. 100; Pavel K, p. 115; Fr_Kosma, p. 124; Dencoy18, p. 133; Oscar C. Williams, p. 135; iconspro, p. 136; Gts, p. 137; Toasted Pictures, p. 140; SusaZoom, sidebar graphic.

Roman road photograph by Bernard Gagnon/Wikimedia.org, p. 79

Hills of Samaria by Cyndi Parker, used by permission, p. 56

Relief maps by Michael Schmeling, www.aridocean.com